Preventing Binge Drinking on College Campuses

A Guide to Best Practices

Toben F. Nelson, Sc.D., and Ken C. Winters, Ph.D.
with Vincent L. Hyman

HAZELDEN®

Hazelden
Center City, Minnesota 55012
hazelden.org

ISBN: 978-1-61649-217-5

Editor's note

The names, details, and circumstances may have been changed to protect the privacy of those mentioned in this publication.

This publication is not intended as a substitute for the advice of health care professionals.

16 15 14 13 12 1 2 3 4 5 6

Cover design: David Spohn
Interior design and typesetting: Madeline Berglund

Contents

Foreword

by Henry Wechsler, Ph.D.

Director of the Harvard School of Public Health
College Alcohol Study and author of *Dying to Drink:
Confronting Binge Drinking on College Campuses*

Heavy alcohol consumption by college students is not a new phenomenon. In colonial days, Thomas Jefferson complained about student drinking at the University of Virginia. At Harvard College in the 1600s, a sheriff was needed to lead the graduation procession in order to control drunk and disorderly persons.

The first large-scale scientific study of college student drinking was published almost sixty years ago by Robert Straus and Selden Bacon in their seminal work, *Drinking in College.* Their survey of twenty-seven American colleges reported heavy drinking among men and somewhat lower drinking rates among women.

In 1993, the Harvard School of Public Health College Alcohol Study examined drinking patterns of over 17,000 students at a nationally representative sample of 140 colleges in 40 states and the District of Columbia. The study found that two out of five college students were binge drinkers (men consuming five or more drinks in a row, and women four or more). Binge drinking had consequences for drinkers, including fights, interpersonal problems, arrests, injuries, and lost educational opportunities. Others in the drinkers' environment were also impacted through secondhand effects such as injuries, verbal assaults, noise, and a degraded living environment.

The results of the Harvard study were reported in 1994. Since then, over one thousand studies on college student drinking have been published in professional psychological, sociological, educational, public health, and medical journals. Heavy drinking by students is recognized today as a serious problem at colleges and is addressed by senior-level administration at most colleges. A number of methods have been developed to address the problem. Individual approaches offer some proof of results. Yet on a national level reports of the current status of drinking in American colleges indicate that little, if any, change in drinking rates has occurred since 1994.

There may be many reasons for the overall lack of change. Foremost may be the tendency for interventions to be one-dimensional—that is, colleges try an educational program, or increased penalties for offenders, or redefinition of drinking norms. These are single approaches to a problem that is multidimensional. Binge drinking in college does not have a single cause and cannot be eliminated by a single solution. The behavior stems from a variety of factors, including the background and history a student brings to college, his or her expectations about drinking at matriculation, the drinking traditions and norms at the school, and the particular setting at the college. This setting may include fraternities, athletics, or an alcohol-free environment; it also includes the alcohol environment in the surrounding community, specifically marketing to students, alcohol pricing, and special promotions.

This book offers the sweeping approach needed to cope with the complex problem of college binge drinking. The authors present a simple way to carry out a research-based strategy for action on a number of fronts. This thoroughly comprehensive guide is an invaluable tool for any college seeking to address the problem of binge drinking by students.

Henry Wechsler, Ph.D.
Quincy, Massachusetts
January 2012

Acknowledgments

This book is the result of experiences that were directly informed by many important people. I am grateful for the opportunity to have worked on the Harvard School of Public Health College Alcohol Study (CAS) and the "A Matter of Degree" (AMOD) program evaluation. This book is a reflection of the many things I learned from my involvement in that project. I am particularly indebted to Henry Wechsler, a kind, brilliant, and visionary man whose work has made an enormous impact on our understanding of alcohol use among college students. I am also thankful for the friendship of Elissa Weitzman, who hired me to work on the AMOD evaluation and gave me an opportunity to develop as a scientist. I miss working with them on a daily basis, as I do my colleagues at the Harvard School of Public Health: Mark Seibring, Alison Diez, Kerry Folkman, Kathy Carrothers, Hang Lee, Meichun Mohler-Kuo, Jae Eun Lee, Karen Powers, Amanda Rudman, and Catherine Lewis. CAS and AMOD were possible through the vision, commitment, and money provided by many very smart folks at the Robert Wood Johnson Foundation, including Joan Hollendonner, Seth Emont, Marjorie Gutman, Dwayne Proctor, Tracy Orleans, and Steven Schroeder. Our colleagues at the American Medical Association—Richard Yoast, Sandra Hoover, and Don Ziegler—deserve thanks for their leadership, hard work, and insights. I also want to thank our AMOD site evaluation staff—Brenda Egolf, Brenda Woods, Laurel Crown, William Lugo, Anne Dorwaldt, Julie Kearney, Duane Shell, Diane Leiva, Steven Martin, Deanna Moore, and Carol Bormann—for being objective observers and reporters, and the program staff and coalition members at the AMOD, of whom there are too many to list. I learned a great deal from each of you.

My colleagues in the Alcohol Epidemiology Program at the University of Minnesota—Traci Toomey, Darin Erickson, Kathleen Lenk, Rhonda Jones-Webb, and Mark Miazga—have helped me develop a new perspective on preventing problems associated with alcohol use and are a wonderful group of people to work alongside. Finally, I want to thank Ken Winters and Vince Hyman. Ken is a terrific colleague who brings an important perspective to complement my own. I enjoyed working with him on this book and look forward to other projects. Vince is a skilled writer and I appreciate his ability to push me to say what I really mean.

—T. N.

I wish to extend a heartfelt thanks to several people who provided support of my work on this project, including my wife, Kate; my core staff at the University of Minnesota (Tamara, Andria, Christine, and Patrick); and my close research colleague, Randy Stinchfield. I also want to acknowledge the guidance and mentorship I received in graduate school from my advisor, the brilliant John Neale, who set me on my research path and who will be greatly missed by all of his mentees. Finally, a personal thanks to Vince Hyman for his outstanding contributions to this effort.

—K.W.

GETTING STARTED

A Complex Problem

As a reader of this book, you are likely already convinced that alcohol use on campus is a serious problem. You recognize that its use damages students' health and safety. It thwarts their success. It harms the college's reputation. It infuriates nearby residents. And yet for many people, excessive drinking also seems to be just part of "the college experience."

Intuitively, you know that your real job is to help open *others'* eyes to this issue. You sense that the problem of binge drinking is a self-perpetuating cycle. As the campus becomes known for drinking, it attracts more "party students." The cycle has to change.

This book will help you make your college community a better one. It will help you in your mission of bringing out the best in the people you serve.

You will learn to find allies, gather them into a more powerful group, show them how to reduce the severity of the problem, and then get to work.

Alcohol use is a serious, complex issue. From a national perspective, research has shown that about two in five college students report binge drinking, defined as five or more drinks in a row for males and four or more drinks for females, in the previous two weeks.[1]

College students drink *more* on average than young adults who do not attend college.[2] When at college, students often live in an environment that makes alcohol and opportunities to drink widely available. Students may also be less accountable for the consequences of their drinking than if they were part of the workforce. This may be why students tend to drink less after graduating, beginning careers, and starting families.

Solid evidence supports the use of specific strategies that can shape the college environment to reduce student drinking and its negative consequences. But colleges and communities have, by and large, not adopted these efforts. Understanding the challenges to enacting these effective and recommended strategies is an important step toward overcoming them.

When we talk to campus administrations across the country, we find that schools share many common concerns regarding alcohol abuse by students. These concerns extend beyond statistics. They include the emotional and physical damages associated with binge drinking, damage to educational advancement, reputational damage, and financial costs.

Though the concerns are deep and real, there is good reason for the relative inaction on most campuses. From an administrative viewpoint, changing the drinking habits at a school can appear to be a lose-lose proposition:

- It costs political capital to change course.
- Some individuals may get upset by anti-drinking initiatives—students, alumni who romanticize their college drinking exploits, and those who sell alcohol.
- There are costs associated with changing the policies, practices, and systems at and around the school. Enforcement, formal screening, brief intervention, training programs, and other such efforts cost money.

This inaction is especially troubling in an era when publicly funded campuses face regular budget cuts, and when, for some students, the cost of a college education is a thirty-year debt.

Yet school leaders can do many things to set the tone for change. The administrator's bully pulpit matters. Many of the changes recommended in this book are not about costs but about realignment and creating synergies among existing activities and stakeholder groups. If you are the administrator, you can lead those changes; if you are a part of a college task force working to change the environment, you can help top leaders see the benefits from taking the risks to change the culture. And you can point out the hidden costs of inaction, such as legal liability for failing to respond to a health issue on campus and damage to the school's reputation—not to mention the human costs of damaged lives, students failing out, and the college's failure at its primary mission of education.

Costs and Benefits

As with any prevention approach, the costs to intervene should be weighed against the costs of failure to intervene. The Lewin Group recently detailed the societal costs of alcohol in the United States.[3] They found that in 2006, the total cost of drinking in the United States was more than $220 billion, or more than $700 for every man, woman, and child. The cost of binge drinking was more than $170 billion of that total. These costs resulted from lost productivity and the expense of providing health care and criminal justice services. Because college students tend to drink more heavily than other groups, their families, colleges, and taxpayers in college communities may bear disproportionately more of these costs.

A cost-benefit analysis at your college would uncover many reasons to institute binge-drinking prevention. The following pages describe in more detail the costs that result from student drinking, including costs not addressed in the Lewin Group report.

Retention

The typical public four-year college or university invests more than $400 per student for recruitment and retention, and a typical private four-year college spends more than $2,000 for each student that is enrolled. The average college can lose one in four students from the first to the second year. That works out to about $100 at a public school and $500 at a private school for each student who starts but doesn't make it to the second year. The longer the student has been involved with the school, the more resources the school has invested in the student. Graduation rates *matter* because they are a primary outcome of college and an indicator of the college's effectiveness. The college had better succeed at it. What might it be worth to increase your four-year graduation rate by 5 percent? 10 percent?

According to a report by Noel-Levitz, a higher-education consulting firm, the average public four-year college spends more than $450,000 for every 1,000 new students enrolled. An average private four-year college can spend more than $2 million for the same return, and these costs are increasing over time.[4] That is a considerable investment considering that (a) the average four-year college retains only about three out of every four students from the first to the second year of college; and (b) only slightly more than half complete their degrees within five years, according to ACT Educational Services. Although many factors can contribute to student retention, alcohol use is an important contributor to whether students continue on to successfully complete their degrees.[5]

In this light, there is every reason to allocate at least part of your budget for student retention to alcohol reduction efforts. Your efforts to reduce student drinking are not simply a cost—they are an investment in improving graduation rates. You no doubt view other efforts to retain students as an investment. Your budget for alcohol reduction efforts is no different.

Thus, one benefit to instituting binge-drinking prevention is improved retention. But there are other important considerations in this cost-benefit analysis.

Reputation

The public relations benefit of avoiding disaster becomes clear when you look at some of the more memorable alcohol-fueled campus fiascoes. A mention of Duke University's lacrosse team still brings shudders to many campus professionals. Though the scandal is now more than six years old—an eternity in the American news cycle—it's still fresh for many on college campuses. The case involved a student at North Carolina Central University who was hired to perform as a stripper at a party for the team at a house owned by Duke University. The young woman subsequently alleged that she was raped by team members who were drunk. Though charges were eventually dismissed, alcohol clearly facilitated a series of poor decisions.

Or consider the riots at the Minneapolis campus of the University of Minnesota. In 2009, students rioted during an annual event called "Spring Jam," tearing down street signs, attempting to flip cars, and harassing drivers. Close to seventy police were required to restore order. Police attributed the riot to alcohol and youthful exuberance.[6] The riot was reminiscent of a similar event six years earlier, when students rioted after the men's hockey team won the NCAA tourney. Rioters set fires, smashed windows and cars, and hurled bottles at police. The student newspaper described it as "an alcohol-fueled frenzy."[7]

The damage to a college's reputation caused by these types of events can take years to overcome.

Promoting Student and Community Well-Being

Limiting alcohol problems can be part of an overall campus effort to develop student assets and values, reinforce the educational mission of the school, and call the student community to its highest aspirations. These efforts can attract positive attention to the campus. A great example is the University of Nebraska–Lincoln (UNL). UNL set out to change its reputation as a drinking school in 1997. By implementing the program model "A Matter of Degree" (AMOD)—supported by the

Robert Wood Johnson Foundation—UNL was successful in making important changes in drinking behavior and consequences at the school.[8] There were reductions of 5 to 18 percent in rates of binge drinking, frequent intoxication, initiation into binge drinking at college, and alcohol-related problems such as missing classes, getting in trouble with police, and getting injured.[9] UNL's success came over a number of years, as leaders worked to improve their counseling and prevention services and change policies at the local and state levels, including a change in state identification cards to decrease the use of false identification, thus reducing underage access to alcohol. UNL's strong media advocacy attracted positive attention to the school for its efforts to improve the welfare of students, including several editorials in the *Lincoln Journal Star* on the benefits of the campus-community coalition.[10] The school received national attention as a result of its success, and its leaders are now recognized as experts in creating campus-community change on student alcohol issues. The recruitment and retention benefits of such attention should not be underestimated. School donors are also positively influenced when a campus sets out to improve the well-being of its student body.

Another example hails from Iowa City, where downtown business owners were fed up with drunken University of Iowa (UI) students who broke store windows, strewed trash, and committed minor vandalism, all of which weakened the already struggling downtown. In 2010, the city created the 21-only ordinance, restricting bar entry to adults age twenty-one and older. Comparing February 2011 to February 2010, officials found that citations for underage drinking dropped 45 percent.[11]

In our view, the most effective binge-drinking reduction programs improve campus-based services and involve the community far beyond the campus. UNL and the efforts of the Iowa City business owners are examples of the benefits of building bridges among multiple stakeholders, and how these connections yield positive outcomes.

Human and Economic Costs

Part of your work will be to determine the human and economic costs to your specific campus. Here are some general facts to help you see the scope of the problem nationally.[12]

- Annual alcohol-related deaths of college students ages eighteen to twenty-four: 1,400.
- Annual alcohol-related injuries among college students ages eighteen to twenty-four: 500,000.
- Alcohol-related physical assaults: 600,000.
- Instances of alcohol-related sexual assault or date rape: 70,000. Alcohol is involved in nine of every ten campus rapes.
- Two in five college students are binge drinkers (defined as five or more drinks for men, four or more for women).
- One in five college students is a frequent binge drinker (three or more binges in a two-week period).
- One in three college students meets official diagnostic criteria for a current (prior twelve months) alcohol use disorder (either abuse or dependence).[13]
- Students are more likely to binge-drink if they are white, age twenty-three or younger, and a resident at a fraternity or sorority.
- Frequent binge drinkers are twenty-one times more likely than non-bingers to be hurt, get in trouble with the police, engage in unprotected or unplanned sex, damage property, fall behind in schoolwork, and miss class.
- Binge drinkers disrupt the lives of their classmates who don't drink or who drink but not at a binge level. Seventy-five percent of these moderate or non-drinkers report these types of experiences caused by drinkers: unwanted sexual advances; physical aggression; insults; property damage; sleep and study time interruptions.

- Students spend $5.5 billion annually on alcohol—more than their combined expenses for books and nonalcoholic beverages.
- The U.S. Department of Justice reports that underage drinking costs more than $58 billion annually; the costs include crime, traffic crashes, treatment, and alcohol poisoning.

CAsE EXAMPLE

HAZING PROVES A PR NIGHTMARE

In December 1999, a University of Vermont hockey player filed suit against members of the athletic department and university administration, alleging failure to respond to a hazing incident that included forced binge drinking and demeaning behaviors. The suit stalled, but the resulting public relations nightmare caused the university to cancel the remainder of the hockey season.

The fallout included more than 73 newspaper articles, coverage in *Sports Illustrated,* and national news coverage. There were 102 letters to the editor, 35 percent of which were critical of the university's handling of the hazing incident, and 46 percent of which were supportive of the university and its athletic programs. For several weeks the event and its aftermath absorbed the time and resources of the president's office, the athletic department, the office of student affairs, legal counsel, and the offices of government and public relations.

The incident shone a light on high-risk drinking as part of hazing, peer pressure, and allied issues. Over the long term, increased resources were put into training around alcohol use and abuse. There was increased communication across the campus and the local community about the dangers of forced drinking in

---

continued on next page

athletics and Greek organizations. And there was more discussion of the accessibility of alcohol, including attention to the use of false IDs and the prosecution of an upperclassman who supplied alcohol to underage team members.

Events like this show the time and resources binge drinking consumes on campus. They also are an opportunity for the campus alcohol coalition to gain ground in publicizing and changing the attitudes and behaviors about alcohol, and the importance of controlling access to it.[14]

Overview: What Works in Reducing Binge Drinking?

Quite a bit is known about what works and what does not work to reduce binge drinking in an individual and across communities. Many different groups of experts have examined the evidence from research and practice to determine the most effective interventions. One group, brought together by the National Institute on Alcohol Abuse and Alcoholism (NIAAA), has collected and evaluated the research that's been done in this area, and it is available at the website www.collegedrinkingprevention.gov. Of special note are the NIAAA's recommendations for substance abuse prevention, adapted below and described as *individual interventions* and *community interventions*.

Individual Interventions

Some strategies to reduce alcohol abuse occur at the individual level—interventions with a student who is already abusing alcohol. The following strategies are considered effective:[15]

1. *Cognitive-behavioral therapy (CBT)*. CBT attempts to change a person's beliefs about alcohol. For college student

programs, CBT typically seeks to change expectations about what will happen as a result of drinking. Training sessions may include documenting a student's alcohol use and teaching stress management. Another element of CBT is norms clarification, which refers to activities that first uncover a student's current perceptions about drinking norms on campus and then challenge those perceptions by explaining the realities.

2. *Brief motivational enhancement interventions.* Motivational enhancement (ME) involves trying to increase an individual's motivation to change behavior. Research shows reduced alcohol consumption among students who receive brief (usually forty-five minutes) motivational enhancement individually or in small groups. The interventions also reduce negative consequences of alcohol, including excessive drinking and driving under the influence.

3. *Challenging alcohol expectancies.* Information and experiential learning are used to alter students' expectations about the effects of alcohol.

The key to successful individual interventions is creating systems and infrastructure on campus to systematically identify those students who need help, and then getting them the appropriate level of help. A 2005 national study found that about one in five students may need some intervention for their alcohol use, but only 7 percent of those students actually receive help. And students don't tend to seek out treatment. Only 3 percent of students who met clinical criteria for an alcohol use disorder sought treatment on their own.[16]

Community Interventions

A second set of strategies has not been specifically researched with students but has been shown to be effective with similar populations.

These strategies are largely aimed at changing access to alcohol in entire communities. They tend to be more effective than individual strategies because they reach many students at once and often involve the surrounding community as well. They change the conditions that influence the drinking behavior of everyone and over time change the cultural norms of a community.

1. *Increased enforcement of minimum drinking age laws.* This is the most well-studied strategy. The NIAAA notes on its website www.collegedrinkingprevention.gov, "Compared to other programs aimed at youth in general, increasing the legal age for purchase and consumption of alcohol has been the most successful effort to date in reducing underage drinking and alcohol-related problems." Increased enforcement via compliance checks at retail alcohol outlets cuts rates of sales to minors by at least half.

2. *Implementation, increased publicity, and enforcement of other laws to reduce alcohol-impaired driving.* Lowering legal blood alcohol content (BAC) limits to .08, and even lower to .02 for drivers under age twenty-one, reduces injury and deaths caused by driving under the influence. Other related laws that have an impact include sobriety checkpoints, server training intervention, and administrative license revocation.

3. *Restrictions on alcohol retail outlet density.* Studies have found a link between the density of alcohol outlets, alcohol consumption, and related violence, crime, and health problems. One study noted by the NIAAA "found higher levels of drinking and binge drinking among underage and older college students when a larger number of businesses sold alcohol within one mile of campus."

4. *Increased prices and excise taxes on alcoholic beverages.* Raising the price is associated with reductions in

consumption and alcohol-related problems. Most studies find that young people are more price-sensitive than the general population. Higher prices are also associated with reductions in traffic crash fatalities and drunk driving, particularly among younger drivers.

5. *Responsible beverage service policies in social and commercial settings.* Training focuses on techniques such as slowing alcohol service, refusing service when a patron has had too much to drink, checking age ID, and detecting false IDs.

6. *Formation of a campus and community coalition involving all major stakeholders to prevent alcohol abuse.* Studies of approaches that involve comprehensive community efforts to reduce alcohol problems have shown that such efforts can be effective. "This approach reframes the issue as a community problem, not simply a college problem, brings together the range of players needed to address it, and sets the stage for cooperative action," reports the NIAAA.

A group of experts convened by the Centers for Disease Control and Prevention (CDC) has recommended a specific set of community-based interventions that have strong evidence supporting their effectiveness.[17] The CDC also provides resources for promoting these changes as well as guidance on how to enact these interventions. Consistent with the NIAAA recommendations, the CDC's Community Guide recommends regulation of alcohol-outlet density, increasing alcohol taxes, and enhanced enforcement of laws prohibiting sales to minors. Additional recommended interventions are

1. *Dram shop liability.* These laws, which can be enacted at the state or local level, hold the owner and/or server at a retail alcohol establishment legally responsible for the harm caused by a customer who was served at that establishment.

Dram shop liability can effectively motivate owners and servers to make sure that their service practices are responsible and that they are not providing alcohol to people under the legal drinking age or who are already intoxicated.

2. *Maintaining limits on the hours and days of sale.* Such laws include state or local laws that restrict the days on which alcohol can be sold (generally Sunday) or that restrict the hours during which retail establishments may sell alcohol on-premises (at bars and restaurants, for example) and off-premises (at liquor stores and grocery stores, for example).

The Community Guide also recommends against privatization of retail alcohol sales in states where the state government has control over at least a portion of the sale of alcohol to the public.

In many instances of these community-based interventions, there has been an erosion of policies that reduce alcohol accessibility. In effect, any positive changes colleges can achieve on their own campus can be overwhelmed by changes in the surrounding environment that ease student access to alcohol.

Very few colleges and college communities have taken steps to adopt these strategies.[18] Of course, these recommendations cover interventions that occur in the community. Such changes cannot be enacted solely by colleges. Colleges are rarely involved in advocating for these policies, but the fact remains that such policies significantly influence student drinking behavior.

However, college administrators represent the campus as members of the community. As such, they can lead change in all of these areas by working with community advocates and people in state and local departments of health. Administrators can actively oppose efforts to weaken these laws where they exist, and mount efforts to tighten these restrictions. Colleges can have a large impact on these debates *if they begin to play a role in them.*

There are many other specific interventions that you can implement on your campus. Whereas some of these have not been rigorously evaluated by research, these additional approaches have enough science to justify their consideration. We recommend that you focus your efforts in the following three areas:

1. Implement a process to systematically screen students for problems with alcohol and a complementary system to ensure that students receive appropriate intervention or treatment.

2. Establish a system for doing quality improvement on existing policies and procedures for addressing student alcohol issues.

3. Advocate for community-based policies and procedures that create an environment that limits excessive drinking.

One area of misunderstanding is the environmental, policy-based approach we recommend in this book. Many college administrators interpret this to simply mean increasing punishment of students. Rather, think in terms of establishing clear standards on your campus and in your community for how alcohol is sold and consumed, and creating ways to hold everyone accountable to those standards. Most policies that are effective in reducing heavy drinking and its negative consequences are aimed at the suppliers of alcohol.

How to Use This Book

This book was written to help the following groups:

- college administrators, faculty, and staff
- boards of regents or others with oversight responsibility for colleges
- students

- parents and families of college students, or soon-to-be college students
- alumni, boosters, and other allies
- local police, courts, health care workers, and others who deal with the ramifications of campus drinking
- neighborhood associations and residents
- city council members, state legislators, and other policy makers
- chambers of commerce and business groups affected by college binge drinking

Our goals for these groups are lofty. In many cases, we may push those involved in the issue beyond their comfort zone. In our view, the fact that colleges have generally not used the strategies we discuss is the reason why there has not been a significant reduction in student drinking and the harm it causes. We believe that by using the tools in this book you can accomplish two very important goals:

1. *In the short term,* you will find a road map to develop and sustain an integrated and multifaceted campus system in which best practices are implemented with respect to policy, prevention, and intervention-related services.

2. *In the long term,* you will reach the ultimate goal—actual reductions in binge drinking among college students and the negative consequences that result.

The Parts of This Book

There are seven chapters to this book, and several documents on the accompanying CD-ROM.

Chapter 1: Getting Started is the chapter you are completing. This chapter provides the rationale for the work you will do. We hope the information on the benefits and costs will help you persuade others to join you in this work and provide you with common language to help advocate for needed change.

Chapter 2: Circles of Influence and Response Model will deepen your understanding of the individual and cultural environment in which alcohol consumption occurs. You will see how state, community, college, and family norms impact an individual student and set the tone for the choices he or she makes. You will gain a deeper understanding of the complexity of people's behaviors around alcohol, and why the environmental approach is critical to changing drinking patterns on campus.

Chapter 3: Laying the Groundwork provides strategies, rationales, and tools for assembling a team to address binge drinking. It covers five steps that will help you begin implementing your plans.

Chapter 4: Implementing a Screening and Intervention System covers the systems the college should have in place to deal with students who are experiencing severe consequences of alcohol use, including addiction.

Chapter 5: Improving the Quality of Policies and Procedures explains the important work the campus must do in "getting its own house in order" before implementing interventions that reach beyond its borders.

Chapter 6: Restricting Alcohol Access illustrates a number of tactics the campus and community can use to change the campus drinking culture. It explains key policies that should be in place as well as how to implement and improve enforcement of policies.

Chapter 7: Influencing Alcohol Prices describes tactics the campus and community can use to end or limit alcohol discounting in the community and raise the price of alcohol. Studies have shown that increased price is directly correlated with reduced consumption, making this a key strategy.

The **Afterword** reminds you of the overarching goals of this book and how the strategies and tactics work together to change the culture of drinking on campus.

The **CD-ROM documents** include assessment instruments, model ordinances, and other useful tools to support your work.

This book follows an arc, beginning with basic grounding in the problems associated with binge drinking, then helping the campus improve its internal systems, and, finally, moving gradually beyond the campus borders into the community. We have intentionally organized the book so that the coalition working on the issue of binge drinking can experience small successes while preparing for the larger, much more effective but also more challenging steps that ultimately will change the culture on campus.

Many of the tools and methods in this book are grounded in public health and clinical scientific research. These resources are not just "good ideas" about what might work. They are tested programs and approaches.

Binge drinking on college campuses seems like an intractable problem. It is not. Drinking occurs in a community environment, and research reveals which elements in the environment are conducive to binge drinking and which elements promote moderation. The environment is a result of many factors—policies, practices, cultural beliefs, and retail economies both on campus and in the surrounding community.

This book will help you see how those elements interact and assist you in devising a process to gradually redirect your college campus system toward a healthier state. Don't expect miracles and don't expect speed. In this effort, patience, persistence, and small wins are what matters. We are talking about cultural change, and such change seems glacial to today's instant-messaging mind-set. But it can be done—and you can do it.

CHAPTER 2

CIRCLES OF INFLUENCE AND
RESPONSE MODEL

F rom abstention to occasional responsible use to binge drinking and addiction, alcohol use on campus occurs in a complex environment. In this chapter, we present a model that will help you think about the shape of this problem. This model, the Circles of Influence and Response Model, can serve as a reference for your campus and community as you develop responses to the problems surrounding alcohol.

Specialists who come to this work wear their own unique set of glasses. The health professional may see a student facing issues of poor nutrition, depression, or unexplained accidents. The addiction professional may see a student struggling with alcohol use. The academic advisor may see a student who has plunged dangerously close to failure. The resident advisor may see a dorm problem. School security may see a threat to public order. The local retail establishment may see a disorderly customer who drives others away. And so on.

None of these pictures is complete. All of them overlook the point that the choice to consume alcohol, and how much alcohol to consume, occurs in a cultural context. The result is that interventions based on one specific perspective miss much of the picture. Because of that, campus specialists risk missing important elements that shape the individual student's behaviors. These include influences of his or her family, current and past friends, and associates on campus. They include the rules, expectations, and covert or hidden norms on campus. They include the consequences the student may face from these and other sources, including the broader community. They include a complex combination of broader community norms, advertising, pricing, public events, and laws at the local, county, and state level.[19]

If you are a drug treatment specialist, you may think that the best intervention for campus alcohol issues is to treat those students who become addicted. Students with a serious drinking problem *do* need treatment, but treating them is not going to address the campus problem. In fact, many points of intervention exist that can help at least some of these students avoid (or delay) the path to addiction, and prevent many more students from binge drinking, experiencing the problems that result, and developing an alcohol use disorder.

The Circles of Influence and Response Model suggests a series of influences and intervention points. This model suggests that the student's experience can be viewed as a series of concentric circles. (See figure 2.1.) Each circle includes a set of influencers and a set of potential interventions.

At the center is the *student*, with the strengths and weaknesses he or she possesses. Next come the student's *family and peers*, then the *campus community*, and, finally, the *broader community* at the regional and state level. Let's look at each of these.

FIGURE 2.1

Circles of Influence and Response Model[20]

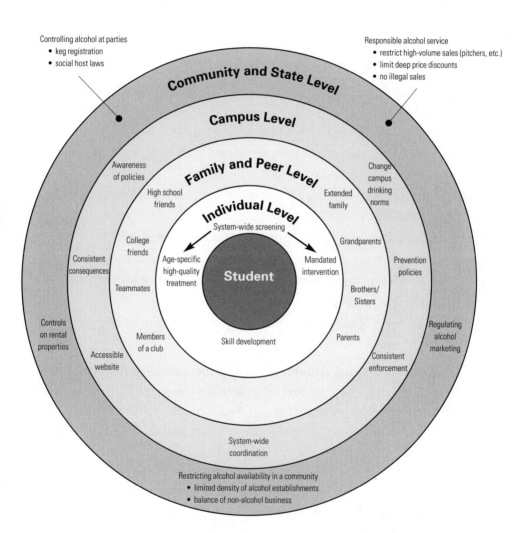

Student (Individual) Level

The student is at the center of the model. He or she can be thought of as having a collection of characteristics that shape behaviors. Here are just a few of these:

- personal drinking and substance abuse history
- familial experiences with alcohol, binge drinking, and addiction
- attitudes and beliefs about alcohol use
- knowledge about the risks associated with heavy alcohol use
- perceptions about what constitutes normative drinking behavior
- predisposition toward binge drinking and other risky behaviors
- predisposition toward resisting peer and other social influences
- access to alcohol (financial resources, transportation, proximity)

Many of the interventions in colleges focus on what happens at this individual level. There are several reasons for this focus. First, many who work on campuses are attracted to the educational environment because they like helping young people learn, develop, and reach their potential. Intervening to improve the life of an individual fits their perception of what they do well, so the approach makes sense. Many schools do an excellent job of helping students understand the risks of alcohol and what can be done to avoid them.

Second, people typically assume that it is easier to change the individual rather than the environment in which his or her problems occur. In practice, it is difficult to change individuals, and there is limited success in doing so on a large-scale basis. Interventions that involve changing the knowledge, attitudes, and practices of those people and institutions that shaped the circumstances in which the student chose to consume alcohol are complicated, may take years to implement, and are difficult to measure. The success or failure of individual interventions is more easily measured and is usually observable within a short time. Also, it can be politically safer to attend to the student's problem rather than focus attention on underlying contextual factors that might influence the student's drinking, such as a problem with family and friends or the presence of a permissive college community.

Each student comes to campus with a unique set of traits and experiences. Researchers do know, however, that there are some typical trajectories that can help predict behaviors once at college. About one in four college students engaged in binge drinking during high school. These youth are very likely to continue binge drinking at college, and their problems associated with alcohol use will most likely escalate. Another group, about one of every four or five students nationally, starts binge drinking upon arrival at campus, although this number can vary widely by college. (This is referred to as the "college effect.")

College officials often focus on the first of these two groups of students, who "bring their drinking habits" to college. In fact, it is very difficult to change the behavior of this group, the members of which have already begun drinking heavily. Only a fraction of these students give up binge drinking in college. It is the second group of students— those who take up binge drinking in college—whose behavior is more amenable to change.

Research with thousands of college students nationally has identified several important factors that seem to facilitate binge drinking in college. Some of these factors are characteristics that students bring with them to college. Males, white students, and those who experimented with drinking in high school were all more likely to binge-drink in college, even if they did not binge-drink in high school. But many important factors in the college environment help facilitate binge drinking in college. These factors include becoming a member of a fraternity or sorority, having easy access to alcohol from another student, being able to get alcohol at a bar or liquor store without proper identification, having access to low-cost alcohol, and attending a school where a lot of binge drinking occurs. These environmental factors are things colleges and communities can influence.[21]

The important point here is that each individual brings a set of traits to college. Colleges can't directly change those traits, but they *can* change other major sources that contribute to college problem drinking. These sources reside within the college and surrounding community, and they can be tapped to deal with student traits. A lot of college administrators get tripped up on this. They say, "Well our students *came here* with heavy-drinking problems—that's why we have the problems we have." The data tell a different story. When effective strategies are endorsed and applied, colleges can make a difference.

Consider this carefully. If colleges could limit the problem to those who arrive with problems—if colleges could reduce the "college effect"—that alone would be a major advance.

Responses at the Individual Level

In studies of binge drinking, researchers have looked at environmental factors and have controlled for the reasonable expectation that certain students select colleges because they have a reputation for heavy drinking. The studies show that the "college effect" is real. Thus, a responsible campus binge-drinking reduction group must look at what it can do to change this effect.

However, on the individual level, there are a range of service-related responses based on the extent of drinking problems experienced by the person. Figure 2.2 provides a visual representation of how drinking involvement and various clinical responses are related. This figure shows a range of clinical responses at the individual level.

FIGURE 2.2

Triangle Framework of Responses for Individuals[22]

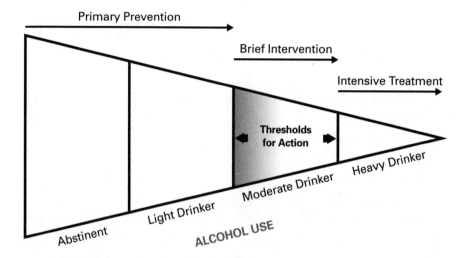

The figure represents the population of college students, partitioned into drinking domains according to level of alcohol consumption and type of health-related response at the clinical level. Level of alcohol consumption is indicated along the lower arm of the triangle. In the United States, there is a segment of the college population that does not consume alcohol, and then there are sizable proportions of college students whose consumption ranges from light to severe. As suggested in the figure, there is a direct relationship between level of alcohol consumption and severity of alcohol *problems.* In other words, the more alcohol a person consumes, the more likely that person will experience problems.

Above the triangle are types of clinical responses by a college as a function of alcohol problem severity. Heavy drinking (typically characterized by frequent binge drinking and meeting clinical criteria for an alcohol use disorder) and the need for intensive treatment primarily occupy the apex of the triangle. Research suggests this is about 5 percent of college students. Most college health service systems are not able to provide intensive treatment for someone with a severe drinking problem, but they likely have the capacity and expertise to provide assessment and referral services for such students. Most college students experiencing this level of a drinking problem do not seek treatment; it is estimated that only 5 percent of students who need help seek treatment and only 3 percent actually get it.[23]

At the individual level, a college health system that provides screening and referral services is providing a meaningful resource to students. Students with less severe alcohol-related problems, characterized by a moderate level of alcohol use (sometimes referred to as *problem drinkers*), occupy a larger proportion of the triangle. Data suggest that about 20 percent of college students meet this category of drinking severity. Perhaps more importantly, a larger proportion of the alcohol-related problems experienced at a given college arise from this group of students. We have identified brief interventions as an appropriate clinical response for such individuals. Some colleges provide this type of service, and, as will be discussed later in this book, several research-based brief interventions programs have been developed for use in college settings.

Randomized studies of individuals who have gone through brief interventions indicate that they can be effective, particularly when the student health system has adequate programs in place to support these services.

Finally, there is a set of students who do not drink or who are light drinkers and have no alcohol problems. For these, prevention services are an appropriate response. Prevention programs focus on educating students to change beliefs, attitudes, and intentions associated with drinking. Note that the success of simply educating students about the risks of binge drinking has been questioned (despite the popularity of educational programs on college campuses), and it is most certainly the case that effective prevention practices require the implementation of environmental-based strategies.

Family and Peer Level

Most college efforts to address student drinking focus on the inner ring of the Circles of Influence and Response Model or, in some cases, the inner two rings. For broader impact on more students, colleges need to move out to the larger circles of influence.

Responses at the Family and Peer Level

Parents today are considerably more involved with their college-aged children than in the past. On campus, students talk to their parents frequently, and parents contact professors and administrators far more than ever. The "helicopter parent" phenomenon is real and extends even to graduate and doctoral students. Research shows that parental attitudes and direction have a strong influence on student behavior, particularly when it comes to drinking. While the influence of parents is strong, it does diminish during college and is replaced by the influence of the student's peers and affiliations. Combined, these constitute the second ring around the student. (See figure 2.1.)

The second circle includes the student's family of origin, peers, dorm mates and classmates, and affiliations with extracurricular and social groups. These influencers are very important. Here is what is known about some of them.

- **Family attitudes** can increase or decrease the likelihood of a student's binge drinking. Students who have parents that model heavy drinking are more likely to drink themselves. The children of parents who disapprove of binge drinking are less likely to engage in binge drinking.[24]

    College programs include policies to notify parents of the extent of binge drinking at colleges and suggest ways they can influence their child's behavior, and parental notification and consequences programs set practices for parental notification if their child is found abusing alcohol (consequences may include expulsion from school, community service, or other consequences of which parents are made aware).

(Admittedly, the data on parental notification programs are not entirely clear. However, researchers have observed that parental disapproval of binge drinking is associated with less student binge drinking. Even among the heaviest student drinkers, only about 2 percent of students reported that their parents had been notified by their school of the student's alcohol violation.[25] Hence the lack of supporting data for this approach may be due to the fact that it hasn't really been tested. We contend that these programs can be successful when a college administers the program consistently.)

- **Peers** influence drinking behavior. People who have friends who binge-drink are more likely to drink heavily, and these friendships often serve as informal networks for accessing alcohol, particularly from those who are of legal drinking age.

  But peers can have a positive influence as well. Peer-helping models include encouraging students to get help for a friend who is experiencing a drinking problem and informing them about what to do when they see a friend "falling-down drunk." An important aspect of these strategies is to get the helper to overcome various disincentives, such as the fear of getting caught for one's own illegal consumption, being disloyal, or damaging the academic success of a friend. Some colleges implement a *medical amnesty policy* that allows the student who is drinking and seeking help for another (in perhaps worse condition) to do so without fear of consequences, although schools can often implement this strategy in practice without adding a formal policy.

- **Greek participation** increases the likelihood of binge drinking. The more engaged students are in Greek life, the more likely they are to drink heavily. Of this group, 70 to 80 percent binge-drink once a week or more often.[26]
- **Athletic** involvement is strongly associated with binge drinking. At the college level, students involved with athletics, whether on a college sports team or with intramural sports, are more likely to drink and more likely to consume larger quantities when they do drink.[27] Perhaps more importantly, because they are a much larger group of students, it is also true for students who are sports fans. About two-thirds of college students were involved as participants in athletics during high school. By college, only about 15 percent of students are on a varsity athletic team, and that number can be much smaller at large schools. Studies show that high school students involved in athletics drink at about the same rate as other high school students. But by the time they reach college, those who participate in athletics during college are more likely to engage in binge drinking, whether they are participating as athletes or fans. Sports clearly have a strong influence on college students' tendency to binge-drink.

Keep in mind that most college campuses focus the intervention on just the individual who is abusing alcohol. But the information above suggests other targets of the intervention. We will explore those next.

Campus Level

At the next circle of influence and intervention is the campus community. You might think of campus-level influences as residing in two basic structures: processes and culture.

The processes involve the development, coordination, and enforcement of campus alcohol policies. They also involve the procedures to enforce those policies and the consequences for violating them. For the most part, the college itself has direct control over these processes at the campus level. (Of course, there are layers of regulation from various government agencies, as well as mandates related to insurers that also shape these processes.)

Second are the less controllable features of the campus environment: its physical layout, location, and proximity to alcohol establishments; and the norms, history, traditions, and myths related to alcohol that together constitute its culture.

It is helpful to think of these formal processes and cultural factors of the college system separately, but in practice, they are not discrete. For example, a college may have strict written procedures and policies, but also a culture of "looking the other way" when it comes time to enforcing the rules among all students or specific subsets of them, such as star athletes. The problem may also be too large and overwhelm any serious effort to monitor and enforce the rules.[28]

These college-level influences are powerful. Consider a young adult who arrives on campus and finds a culture in which upperclassmen mythologize binge drinking. The new student perceives that binge drinking is common and expected, a form of bonding, a way of establishing identity, and largely tolerated by the culture of the college's systems. If that young adult has the normal and developmentally appropriate insecurities, binge drinking can seem like a reasonable, rational thing to do. And it may in fact have some important social benefits. This is simply another way of describing the "college effect." The same young adult arriving at a college that has very high abstinence rates may be less likely to experiment with binge drinking while in school. Clearly, this is not just about an individual student making choices. The college, through its culture, plays an important role in the student's drinking behavior, as do family of origin and peers.

The "map" of campus systems varies, but typically includes

- leadership, including the board of regents and president's office
- administrative offices, including senior administration, office of student affairs, housing, Greek affairs, judicial affairs, office of general counsel, and community relations
- student health services, including direct service provision of prevention, education/awareness, screening, brief intervention, and referral to treatment
- athletic department
- campus police or security
- alumni groups

The map of the culture within the campus systems is not as easy to pin down. Such a map would consist of

- the stories and myths told about drinking experiences by students and alumni
- the school's reputation among students
- the existence, consistency, and longevity of prevention and intervention efforts
- the existence and consistency of consequences and their enforcement
- the overt and covert attitudes about alcohol use and alcohol-related problems as demonstrated in the actions of the people who enforce school policies

All of the factors identified in the two lists above help create the context for student drinking at your campus and are potentially modifiable in terms of the way issues related to student drinking are practiced and communicated. Carefully assessing each of these areas can provide some of the flavor that makes your campus unique in its approach to student drinking issues. And by conducting a careful assessment, you can start to identify areas where the practice is not what you might hope for, and where improvements can be made. The other critical piece is how these different systems function together. It is sometimes easy for students to "fall through the cracks" between these different systems. The good news is that with some intention and effort it is possible to keep this from happening.

Responses at the Campus Level

Students' alcohol use often first comes to the attention of university officials through the staff of campus residential settings—typically, resident assistants and professional housing staff. Those campus professionals end up dealing with alcohol-related incidents, including vandalism, loud parties, and sexual assaults. Campus security also intersects here at times, because the resident assistant's immediate backup is often campus security. These systems work together. Depending on the specific case, responses might occur at the following points:

- *Student affairs.* This may involve a judicial process with the vice president of student affairs office, the dean of students, etc. There may be a formal hearing, and there may be separate but parallel processes for regular students, for students in the Greek system, and for students in athletics. Sometimes these approaches are not consistent, and there are students who get preferential treatment. In some schools, only the worst offenders go through a formal system of intervention and potential expulsion. Other schools have a "three strikes and you're out" system.

- *Health services.* Students on some campuses get routine intake screening that includes alcohol use assessment. Health visits for other reasons may reveal information related to alcohol use. Students may also be referred (via another intervention point) for counseling and additional assessment for alcohol-related problems.

- *Campus security and community police.* On most campuses, there are sworn officers and a campus police force. Others may have security that works closely with the local community police. Typical interventions depend on the situation, but may include a warning, an incident report, a citation, and sometimes an arrest. If a student is arrested, he or she typically goes through both the local judicial process and the campus's internal judicial process.
- *Advisors and faculty members.* Faculty may see the student is having a problem and encourage him or her to seek help. This is more common for mental-health-related issues, but can be capitalized on for alcohol issues as well.

Policies, procedures, and enforcement cut across all the systems above and represent opportunities for the college binge-drinking task force to intervene in the culture of the school by regulating official response to alcohol use, accessibility, and marketing. These interventions eventually directly affect the student (at the center of the Circles of Influence and Response Model) by changing the patterns of response among those who intervene with the student.

Community and State Level

The outermost circle of influences is populated by the systems and culture of the community directly surrounding the campus, as well as its home county and state. These influences (and opportunities for response) are important because, for the most part, colleges don't provide alcohol to students. Usually students obtain alcohol through community sources. These influences and opportunities are frequently overlooked by campus binge-drinking reduction processes. That's unfortunate, because alcohol marketing and accessibility (its price, taxation, and the ease of access to retail outlets) have a major influence on consumption.

When alcohol is too expensive and/or too hard to get, consumption decreases. This is especially true for populations that are very sensitive to price, like college students.

Responses at the Community Level

The influences and opportunities for response at the community and state level include the following:

- *The residential environment.* Alcohol use at off-site student housing can become more of a community problem. How engaged are the landlords in the off-site housing? Do they attend to or ignore problems and complaints? How does the campus work with local neighborhood associations? Are there private, unregulated dorms that serve as apartment buildings for students?

- *Community awareness and level of outrage about students creating a ruckus.* This factor influences how the problem is perceived and how it is dealt with.

- *The nature of the surrounding neighborhood.* In transient and low-income neighborhoods, the community members may not have the political clout to make a difference with their complaints as compared to residents in established, higher-income neighborhoods.

- *Health resources in the community.* Often campuses will not have sufficient resources to provide intervention and treatment services for students. When this is the case, students may be referred to community-based resources. Students may be sharing treatment with people with whom they have little in common, and may feel they don't belong there. The services provided may not be designed for or relevant for a college student.

- *The legal and regulatory environment.* What are the laws and restrictions governing alcohol use and the policies and enforcement resources dedicated to those? For example, as noted in chapter 1, downtown Iowa City, which had a history of troubles with University of Iowa students, reduced underage alcohol use citations 45 percent by enacting a bar entry law. Other modes of influence and intervention include keg registration, keeping a lid on alcohol outlet density, enforcement of compliance checks and legal alcohol sales in licensed establishments, and DUI checkpoints.

- *Distribution.* The number and proximity of alcohol retail outlets influence drinking behavior. For example, the University of Wisconsin–Madison, which is located near a great number of bars, has a high rate of binge drinking. This kind of access is quite typical in Wisconsin, which is also a high-consumption state.

- *Cost.* Alcohol prices are set by retailers and wholesalers, but taxes can increase the cost of alcohol. Discounting (a feature of marketing) and events-related price cuts also influence consumption. Alcohol wholesalers work on a volume business within a geographic territory, and their task is to move more product in their region. They are aggressive behind the scenes.

- *Alcohol marketing.* The presence of billboards, alcohol-sponsored events, and even alcohol-manufactured "prevention" campaigns can increase consumption. Localized point-of-sales advertising, neon signs, and other highly visible sources are one form of influence (and locus for intervention). But alcohol marketing is more pervasive. Does the school newspaper allow bars to run ads? Do campus bulletin boards have informal ads? What about social marketing?

Local law enforcement can be a critically important ally when trying to map the influences and intervention points among students. Officers will likely be able to quickly name the establishments where most cases occur, and provide supporting data. Moreover, community-based police officers can work to develop relationships with the owners of these establishments, which can be very helpful when the campus stakeholders group works to change the local environment.

The policy environment that shapes the community surrounding a campus is complex. Document 1: Effectiveness of Alcohol Policies on the accompanying CD-ROM includes a list of more than forty policies enacted at the state level. Experts have rated each policy as to its effectiveness in changing alcohol consumption patterns. These policies formally codify community standards about how alcohol is marketed, sold, and consumed. The policies also identify the ways in which people who sell and consume alcohol can be held accountable to those community standards.

The importance of local and state policy is often underappreciated by college personnel who work on student alcohol issues. Don't overlook policy. The alcohol control policies that operate in your community and state set the tone for how alcohol is used. These have a dramatic influence on the drinking behavior at your school. Understanding these can help communities reinvigorate efforts to maintain community standards and identify gaps in community standards that can be closed.

Finally, it is useful to be aware of the influence environmental factors have at the community and state level and how those conditions influence risk for alcohol-related problems at the individual level. Figure 2.3 represents an integration of eleven major theoretical streams to demonstrate how drinking behavior is influenced by a complex interaction of individual, social, and economic factors. The historical, physical, and social contexts of both communities and campuses set the environmental conditions that influence alcohol use. These include the availability of alcohol (e.g., number of alcohol establishments surrounding the campus, non-commercial or social sources of alcohol); how alcohol is marketed and advertised; the unit price of alcohol; alcohol control policies, which may exist at multiple levels (e.g., state, local, and campus); and the degree of policy enforcement. These are the conditions that shape how individual students make choices about whether and the extent to which they engage in drinking behavior. An individual student's tendency to engage in drinking behavior is influenced by his or her own personal characteristics and drinking history as well as these environmental conditions. Individual-level perceptions regarding environmental conditions may mediate the influence of environmental conditions. Finally, drinking behaviors influence the experience of various drinking-related harms.[29]

FIGURE 2.3

Integrated Framework of College Drinking Behavior[30]

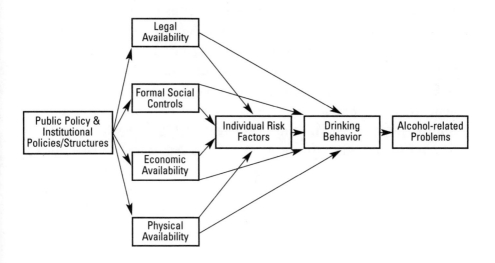

In this book, we recommend that colleges and college communities simultaneously employ two types of approaches to reduce student drinking and the problems associated with it: an approach focused on individual students and an approach focused on the environmental conditions that shape the behaviors of everyone. To some who have worked exclusively on individual approaches—the predominant way of dealing with student drinking issues—it may appear that the environmental approach conflicts with the individual approach and that one has to be chosen over the other. We disagree; our view is that both approaches are necessary.

A word of caution: Calling an intervention "environmental" does not make it environmental. There has been a strong push over the past decade for colleges and college communities to implement environmental interventions. This has encouraged many colleges to start calling the interventions they pursue "environmental" whether they truly are environmental or not. But calling things environmental does not improve their effectiveness. The term "environment" is so vague it invites redefinition. So let us be clear. By *environmental,* we mean the conditions that shape the availability of alcohol in your community. It does not mean rebranding informational interventions, campaigns to educate students about what the normative patterns of drinking for this age group are, or outreach to groups of students in different settings as "environmental." Alcohol-free activities are not environmental interventions. They don't change the availability of alcohol.

Improving the systems for delivering individual interventions is very important, although it is not an "environmental" strategy either. *Do* work to improve the systems for individual intervention delivery. *Do also* pursue environmental interventions *that work,* including the approaches we highlight above. This is not to discourage your campus from pursuing these other interventions. But make sure you are also pursuing interventions that influence the availability of alcohol in your community.

Chapter Summary

The Circles of Influence and Response Model is an orienting framework. Its primary use is to help you understand the complex forces that eventually influence an individual student's choice to consume alcohol, and the degree to which he or she will consume. The model helps you realize the degree to which the modifiable factors in the school and local community can begin to influence student behavior and prevent poor choices.

The Triangle Framework of Responses for Individuals helps you see the distinction between preventive interventions and treatment interventions, and also how they can complement each other.

The Integrated Framework of College Drinking Behavior helps you envision the larger social and environmental influences on drinking behavior and how they create the conditions for making poor or healthy choices about alcohol. These factors have been repeatedly shown to drive patterns of behavior within populations.

Our model and supporting frames of reference are not perfect representations of the problems associated with alcohol use on campus. But they can help frame a systematic response. The way you and others on campus and in the community view the issue of student drinking strongly influences what you do about it. If one views alcohol use solely as an individual choice and individual problem, the response will likely be to focus solely on providing interventions that range from basic education to long-term treatment, depending on the severity of the problem. These responses are important and should be available through health professionals on campus, whether provided directly on campus or via community resources.

However, alcohol abuse, though engaged in by the individual, occurs in an environment that includes the people, policies, processes, and traditions on the campus, in the nearby community, and the state and region. Increasingly, the research shows that colleges and communities can have an impact on the individual's choice and behaviors *by changing the conditions in the environment* that influence these choices. Changing the environment using the strategies we discuss in this book has the potential to impact many more people than individual interventions alone. *Both* approaches are important for college campuses. Colleges and the communities where they are located have been reluctant to adopt an environmental approach, but adding these strategies to existing efforts on campus holds the promise of truly changing binge-drinking traditions on campus.

In many campus prevention efforts, there's a huge disconnect between the people on campus who want to do positive things for students directly and the goal of creating an environment that changes the behavior of the student body. It can be more rewarding and more immediately gratifying to focus on the details of what one student needs, but treating one individual, though absolutely essential for that person's well-being, will not change a culture that encourages binge drinking.

The conflict between these approaches generates a lot of discussion about the relative merits of various interventions. Some interventions *are* better than others. However, campus prevention committees can quickly get bogged down in arguments about whether intervention A is better than intervention B. We suggest that you focus on multiple impacts (A *and* B), and use the research to choose among the most effective interventions.

CHAPTER 3

LAYING THE GROUNDWORK

The recommendations in this book are based on theory, scientific research, and many years of experience observing and working with colleges and communities. Unfortunately, there are many more examples of failures than successes.

There is no need to reinvent the wheel (or the flat tire, in the case of popular interventions that repeatedly fail). On your campus, you can build on insights developed over time and come closer to getting it right for your students. This chapter outlines some advice based on observations working with many campuses and communities across the country. These basic lessons can get you started. The first section will provide more details to keep your effort going.

Make a Commitment to the Strategies That Work

The first step is to commit to the approaches that are highly effective. Below is a list of five overarching strategies. In our view, these strategies constitute the broad outline for a work plan for any campus committed to reducing binge drinking and its related harms. We believe these strategies are necessary and essential. The priorities, tactics, and implementation approaches will vary greatly from one campus and community to the next, but the strategies should not.

- **Strategy 1**: Implement a screening and intervention system on campus to identify and help students who experience problems related to their drinking. This strategy addresses the most troubled students; it ensures that those most at risk for problems to themselves and others receive a quality intervention. (This strategy is discussed in chapter 4.)

- **Strategy 2**: Improve campus policies and procedures for addressing student alcohol issues. This strategy addresses the campus's systems for dealing with alcohol and student use of alcohol. Through this strategy, the college makes sure that the most effective policies and processes are in place. This helps ensure that all students are dealt with fairly, that no students fall through the cracks, and that policies and procedures are aligned efficiently and consistent with the evidence on what works. (This strategy is discussed in chapter 5.)

- **Strategy 3**: Limit the availability of alcohol by reducing marketing, reducing outlet density, and improving responsible beverage service standards. This strategy addresses the accessibility of alcohol by influencing changes in sales promotion and sales procedures. It also moves the campus toward influencing the community that surrounds it. (This strategy is discussed in chapter 6.)

- **Strategy 4**: Enforce existing policies on underage drinking, service to intoxicated patrons, and alcohol-impaired driving. This strategy leverages the existing framework of laws and regulations that operate in most communities, many of which are unenforced, laxly enforced, or inconsistently applied. (This strategy is also discussed in chapter 6, as policy and enforcement work together.)

- **Strategy 5**: Increase the price of alcohol through taxes and by eliminating price discounting. This strategy uses price increases to address the accessibility of alcohol on campus and in the nearby community. The research is clear: alcohol consumption decreases as price increases. Strategies to keep alcohol prices from being too low are among the most effective for reducing binge drinking. This strategy moves the campus beyond its standard comfort zone and into influencing the community. (This strategy is discussed in chapter 7.)

Strategies 1 and 2—implementing a system for screening and intervention and quality improvement of campus policies and procedures for addressing student alcohol issues—focus on your campus and are a good place to start. These are necessary initial steps. However, the evidence is clear: binge drinking is a public health issue. For the vast majority of students, the choice to binge or not is influenced by the availability of alcohol and the accepted standards for its sale and use. Other than those students who may be addicted to alcohol (or on their way to addiction), the evidence is clear that most students *will* shift their drinking behavior in response to alcohol availability and community standards. The only way to change a culture from one that facilitates heavy drinking to one that discourages it is by actively addressing the larger environment. The campuses where binge drinking is common share a culture in which alcohol is cheap and readily available, and in which its harmful consequences are incorrectly attributed to youthful fun. Properly applied, these strategies will help your campus shift from relying on systems to deal with a problem *after* it has already occurred. In effect, you'll be turning off the problem at its source, upstream, rather than trying to play catch-up downstream. This shift may be difficult and is a question of magnitude, but the potential to positively impact students who have not yet set foot on your campus is real and large.

College professionals have historically been reluctant to take on strategies that involve changing the environment—especially when those strategies mean influencing the community that surrounds the campus. Committing to these community strategies may be the most challenging part of making them happen. In fact, colleges have been delaying work on these strategies for fifteen to twenty years, and they have made little progress in reducing student drinking during that time.

While colleges have been hoping for other strategies to work, some things have changed since the mid-1990s. Back then, tobacco use among college students was high and actually rising, despite the declining trends in the population nationally. In the mid-2000s tobacco use among college students dropped substantially. The reason: more campuses stopped selling tobacco products to students in convenience stores and unions on campus as colleges adopted policies that restricted where tobacco could be used. These policies on campus followed tobacco restrictions in workplaces, communities, and states. The adoption of restrictive policies on tobacco was undoubtedly helped by educational efforts to discourage tobacco use and intervention efforts to help with cessation, but ultimately the policies are responsible for the decreased availability of tobacco that, in turn, drove down its use.

Colleges need to apply the same principles to alcohol. The approaches we recommend in this book can help you make that happen.

It is true that colleges cannot take on these issues alone. One reason why colleges have not pursued community-based interventions is that college leaders feel like such interventions fall outside their direct influence. But colleges *can* take leadership in advocating for change in the community. This will not only benefit them, but will benefit the community as well. This book walks you through a variety of ways to influence the campus and communities in ways consistent with the five strategies just listed. This chapter focuses on the *precursors* to carrying out the strategies: assembling the key stakeholders and gathering the most useful information to help build your case for change.

The steps to ready your campus include the following:

Step 1. Assemble a team made up of a broad set of people with a stake in the issue.

Step 2. Educate the group about the problem of binge drinking. This will ensure that group members share a similar perspective grounded in evidence about the factors that influence student drinking, and what works (and what doesn't) to change those factors.

Step 3. Assess the team's capacity to do the work, and be sure you've recruited the skills that you need.

Step 4. Assess the alcohol environment on campus and in the surrounding community.

Step 5. Choose a set of evidence-based strategies and devise a plan for implementation (addressed in subsequent chapters).

Step 1. Assemble a Team

Once you have committed to the specific strategies we recommend, you need to build the infrastructure to make them happen. This means pulling together a group of people who have the right perspective and skills to implement these interventions. Many campuses already have a group devoted to addressing student alcohol problems. Some will be assembling one for the first time. The following advice applies to either situation.

We recommend a two-part structure consisting of a **task force** (or **coalition**) led by a **steering group.** The task force can be quite large, welcoming a comprehensive membership of people concerned about alcohol use by students on and off campus, including campus stakeholders, community stakeholders, and others (although the group may want to exclude people who are part of the alcohol distribution system). The smaller (five to seven members) steering group's role is to set the strategies and guide the work of the coalition.

In practice, campus alcohol coalitions quickly become big, broad, and unfocused. Typically a number of well-meaning people join, and, after observing a few meetings, some begin to delegate attendance to subordinates. The coalition quickly becomes bogged down as members come and go, meeting time is spent introducing new members, and people lose passion and energy and feel that their time is being wasted. In addition, coalitions tend to get overpopulated with campus representatives, and lack adequate membership from important community groups such as the neighborhood association, police-community liaison, chamber of commerce, and so forth. Whether campus- or community-based, most stakeholders come with their own particular set of assumptions—perhaps seeing students as neighborhood troublemakers, as people who need medical treatment, or as customers. Stakeholders also come with biases about which approaches will best solve the problem.

It is very difficult to make decisions with such a group. The cumbersome nature of the group is just one problem. Another is the loss of commitment and passion that occurs when a "pet" solution is not favored (or is shown, through research, to be ineffective). The result can be infighting, endless debate over which single solution is the best, and dysfunction.

Yet a large-scale change in the campus and community environment requires broad participation and buy-in. It needs a lot of horsepower. And the horses need to pull in generally the same direction.

This is why we recommend the two-part structure. The small steering group meets frequently, sets strategy, and then keeps the larger coalition moving in the same direction while permitting a range of solutions that appeal to various coalition members—thus keeping them motivated and involved.

Steering Group

Before we turn to the membership of the task force, let's address the nature of the steering group. The committee should be small—five to seven members—so that it can make decisions nimbly. Members should

- be politically savvy
- have a broad view about the public health problems

associated with drinking—see it as a large, cultural issue rather than simply a problem of individual misbehavior or health
- have power and authority to make and implement decisions among their particular constituency
- control or have access to control over funding and other resources

People who hold some of the following positions would typically be members of the steering committee.

College President, Chief of Staff, Provost/Vice Provost, or Dean of Student Affairs

A person from this positional level should be a key and passionately committed member of the group. It's critically important that high-level leadership buys in and does some of the legwork (that is, does not delegate these activities). The membership of a person at this level sends a message that addressing binge-drinking problems is a high priority for the school. A person at this level can use his or her positional authority to reach trustees, alumni, donors, local and state government leaders, and other leaders. This member can also use positional authority to bring the school's concern to peers in other institutions.

Chief of Campus Security

In many cases, campus security (or campus police) is the system that confronts student drinking issues most directly. It is often the first group to identify students in trouble. Good procedures must be in place to help campus security link those students into other campus systems, including judicial, counseling, and health systems, as well as resources in the local community. The chief of campus security should have strong ties to community police. Actions might include coordinating enforcement efforts with local police, establishing and improving procedures for data collection, and ensuring that high-risk students who get involved with the police don't get lost between systems.

Local Neighborhood Association Leader

Neighborhoods are affected by the campus and need a clear voice. The neighborhood perspective is often missed on campus, yet it is very important, as residents surrounding the campus have considerable influence over the regulatory bodies that affect the campus environment. As a member of the steering group, this person's role is to remind the steering group of the things that are happening out in the community and the potential interventions that can take place there. This person can make connections with students living in the neighborhood, and get those students involved in positive neighborhood activities. This member will also be able to bring the campus's internal concerns out to the community while primarily advocating for community issues. Typically, this person can quickly find out where the problem houses or who the problem landlords are. And this person can mobilize community members to encourage local authorities to pass new ordinances, increase enforcement, and make other changes to help contain heavy drinking by students.

Elected Official

This could be the mayor of the city, a city council member, or sometimes the legislator who represents the area. The person should recognize that student drinking is an important political community issue. This person brings some of the same clout as the neighborhood representative and can push an agenda in local legislation/local ordinance. Even if your group doesn't include an elected official, you should seek the ear of such a person, or a reasonable substitute, such as the mayor's chief of staff. In our experience working with colleges, those steering committees that involve local elected officials were more active in the community, so such membership is a definite benefit.

Campus Health Leader

The person responsible for student health is usually the point person when a student experiences health consequences from alcohol consumption.

This person is also likely to interface with the local emergency room, detox center, or treatment facility. Student insurance is often run through the campus health office. On some campuses, prevention initiatives and treatment activities are handled together. However, there is a risk that health services (medical or mental health) will continue to focus solely on individual problems, missing the larger public health issue and the opportunity for environmental interventions that can prevent more students from experiencing negative consequences. This narrow focus has been responsible for derailing efforts to pursue more effective environmental initiatives, particularly if it pushes the steering committee toward an exclusive strategy of individual counseling interventions. For this reason, when a campus health person is involved, be sure that he or she is on board with the larger environmental approach to this problem.

Steering Committee Organizer

It helps if the committee can appoint a part-time or full-time person to run the stakeholder group meetings, coordinate its work, and convene (but not lead) the steering committee. Such a person should have community organizing skills. He or she should know how to drive public opinion, generate support, mobilize supporters, use social networking systems, and recruit and socialize with the right people. Ideally, the individual will also bring a strong public health perspective. This person should be running the task force. Characteristics of this person should include: established political connections and experience, such as working on a campaign at any level; the ability to work with a diverse range of people comfortably; formal training or background in public health; administrative skills; or training in community organizing, campaigning, or issue-based advocacy.

Faculty Member

Faculty members can bring useful academic expertise to the committee. Though this might be someone from the psychology department, we recommend that you think more broadly; consider someone from political science, sociology, anthropology, public affairs, or the law school. This should be someone who is invested in the issue and ideally brings some expertise that the task force can use. He or she could be skilled in data analysis and interpretation. This group member could influence the advisor/advisee relationships among faculty and students to funnel students who have problems with alcohol to the appropriate intervention services. (Research shows that among students who have signs and symptoms of needing intervention, those who have a close faculty mentor are more likely to seek and receive treatment if they need it.) Faculty members often provide the adult influence that can help students gain insight and perspective into their drinking behavior.

A Cautionary Note: Student Member

Steering groups are often tempted to include a student member on the committee. We recommend proceeding with caution for several reasons. Student perspective is limited by their brief life experience. Student-appointed leaders often come from the heavy-drinking groups—the highly social groups, fraternity or sorority crowd, athletes—who may not understand the full student body they represent. Because of that, they often will advocate for and pursue interventions that aren't likely to work or have a broad impact. Finally, student representation tends to shift frequently, while the campus initiative will evolve over many years. For these reasons, we suggest using students on the stakeholder group, but not as part of the steering committee.

A good steering committee can facilitate and mobilize the work of a much larger task force. The steering committee is where the deep commitment to the recommended strategies must develop and be sustained. The next section describes how the task force can be populated and the relationship between its work and the work of the steering committee.

Steering Group Candidates

The steering group should consist of five to seven people who

- ▶ are politically savvy
- ▶ believe that binge drinking is a public health issue that requires a public health solution
- ▶ have power and authority to make and implement decisions
- ▶ control or have access to control over funding or other resources

Likely candidates:

- ▶ College president, chief of staff, provost/vice provost, or dean of student affairs
- ▶ Chief of campus security
- ▶ Local neighborhood association leader
- ▶ Elected official
- ▶ Campus health leader
- ▶ Steering committee organizer (part-time to full-time position)
- ▶ Faculty member

Relationship between the Task Force and Steering Committee

The task force should be much larger than the steering committee. Its members will have diverse and often contradictory viewpoints. Yet these people can work on their disparate goals while a broader strategic direction is pushed forward. For example, each participant in the task force can identify gaps and areas for improvement within his or her control, take accountability for those, and report back to the larger task force group. These small, local quality-improvement efforts can be important. The larger task force can facilitate them through encouragement and help those leading these smaller efforts to be held accountable to the larger group. But a large task force is not necessary to make many of these smaller changes. They should not distract the group from pursuing more substantive change.

The other value of the task force is that people begin to communicate across the table about the same problem. This brings to light new opportunities. It also has the very practical purpose of helping to keep individual students from falling through the cracks in the intervention system. For example, the housing department can alert the counseling department about a student's alcohol use, and so forth. The task force can gradually tighten up the different systems across the campus and into the community. A series of individual interventions that function synergistically can contribute to a new cultural norm that discourages alcohol abuse.

Often, a large task force can get bogged down in the details of operations of existing systems, missing the recommended larger environmental changes. Members may see that many of the environmental changes—for example, increasing taxes on alcohol sales to make alcohol more expensive for students—appear beyond their control. However, the steering committee can coordinate the efforts of the task force toward improvements in systems and procedures while pursuing a comprehensive strategic plan for accomplishing the larger environmental changes, such as eliminating price specials or other efforts to raise local excise taxes. When it's time to mobilize the full force of the stakeholder group toward this action, the group will be ready.

Focus is critical. The steering committee should choose a primary strategy on which to focus (say, raising excise taxes) and encourage task force members to support that strategy. But behind the scenes, it might also be working to get compliance checks at retail outlets and conduct server training. The task force, meanwhile, focuses on the primary strategy and making connections to be sure the gaps are eliminated.

Task Force Membership

Your campus may already have a stakeholder group committed to dealing with binge drinking. If so, use the list below to assess your current membership and consider additions and changes. In general, you want members who

- are committed to and passionate about the issue
- want to understand the issue
- want to improve things within their own purview and within the larger environment
- have decision-making power within the area they represent
- are open to the environmental/public health framing of the issue

Members of the steering committee also serve on the task force. Be inclusive of the campus and community, but think carefully about how the task force is populated and how the people who join can work together productively. The entire plan can be derailed by people who don't understand the bigger environmental issue that is shaping student behavior or by people who don't want to make changes that involve policy, enforcement, accountability, and sometimes punishment of students and those who provide them with alcohol.

Typical membership of the task force may include the following:

Campus members

- Members of the steering committee
- President (or his or her representative)

- Representative of the board of regents (or someone at the board level)
- Administrators, such as provost, vice provost, vice president of student affairs, dean of students, health services director, director of housing, director of external relations (alumni outreach), development person. The members can help with community outreach and allay concerns that donors will be reluctant to give if the alcohol culture is disturbed.
- Athletics, Greek affairs, law enforcement, campus security, director of recreational services/student union, student organization director, intramural program
- Student health service
- Faculty
- Student representatives

Community members
- Mayor, city council
- Local police department head or sheriff
- Alcohol beverage control agency
- Department of public safety
- Legislators (or their staffers) who are supporters of the university (especially if you are at a state school)
- Local health care (administrative or data side from the local emergency room or detox center, which may encounter students with alcohol issues)
- Local health department (which will have local data, a public health perspective, and experience working on similar public health issues in the community)
- Neighborhood associations
- Alcohol establishment owners, if they truly want to contribute to the solution, can help with credibility with

the larger group and bring a useful perspective. Their membership can help counter the charge that this is a neo-prohibitionist effort. (However, see our warnings about the involvement of the alcohol industry in chapter 7, especially the case example How the Alcohol Industry Derails Alcohol Prevention on page 179.)

- Alumni and parents of students
- Local treatment community representatives, if they represent an organization to which students are typically referred from campus

Updating an Existing Alcohol Coalition

In many cases, the college already has a task force committed to reducing alcohol problems on campus. In these cases, it's essential that you re-examine your membership to be sure you have the forces you need. In our experience, many campus coalitions err on the side of too many college staff and student members and too few community members. This creates two problems: (1) it can cause the coalition to turn in the direction of only addressing individual-level interventions (dealing only with the students assessed to have alcohol abuse issues); and (2) it insulates the college from the community, making success with the environmental strategies less likely.

Efforts to update an existing coalition can be done in combination with step 3—when the task force assesses its capacities and resources (see page 62). The exercise Assessing Representation can help.

Exercise: Assessing Representation

Create a large "concentric circles" model (based on figure 2.1). Post this in the group's meeting space.

Then, as a group, list the various *actions* the task force is taking to address alcohol problems within each circle. Also list which task force *member organization* is leading each action.

- ▶ Student

- ▶ Peer

- ▶ Family

- ▶ Other adults

- ▶ Campus systems

- ▶ Community

- ▶ State

This simple exercise will help you see where your energies and coalition members are focusing. As you seek new members, specifically seek those who will populate the empty circles. Also find out which members are interested in shifting their attention to a new circle.

Group Meetings

Both the steering committee and the task force should meet regularly. The steering committee needs to stay on top of the progress being made toward the overarching strategies—through the work its own members are doing as well as through the efforts of the larger coalition. The steering committee should also discuss ways to gently guide the task force in the right direction—toward the public health agenda. Steering committee members (and not their appointed representatives) should also attend the regular task force meetings.

The steering committee organizer (someone who can devote considerable time to the effort, perhaps even a full-time person) should coordinate the agendas for the steering committee and the task force. The task force should meet regularly, have an agenda and goals that are spelled out and distributed in advance, and conduct its work through subcommittees that it sets up to accomplish actions. It should focus its meetings on subcommittee reports about actions accomplished, holding itself (and members) accountable for goals set and implemented, and ongoing education of the members regarding binge-drinking issues and interventions.

As noted, the task force can suffer if it is dominated by campus people. For this reason, arrange to meet off campus on occasion. This sends a message that the group values the off-campus partners. It brings the issue into the community.

Pulling Weeds and Herding Cats

Sometimes it becomes clear that a task force member is not contributing to or, worse, is derailing your efforts. You may need to ask people to leave if their actions are truly counterproductive. However, often you can occupy less productive members with tasks that are consistent with their personal interests but that don't distract from the big

continued on next page

picture. For example, the research shows that alcohol-free events for students are usually attended by students who would not otherwise drink and don't really help to change the drinking environment on campus. A student or a few advocates may still be convinced that this is the one best approach. Rather than expending energy blocking them, let them follow their course, but don't let them distract the group. No damage will be done by such an event, and you can simply let them report back to the group on the outcomes of their actions.

Simultaneously, set in motion a plan to recruit new, more suitable members. Ground the recruitment plan in your strategic agenda (for example, cessation of discounting, increase in alcohol excise taxes, and implementation of mandatory responsible beverage training). Bring in the new forces you need and don't worry about the rest unless they are actively sabotaging your agenda.

If you focus too much energy on ensuring that everyone is aligned on the same tasks or on finding the "right" solution, you'll be locked in eternal, energy-sapping debate. Don't let that happen. Let three or four members who want to do something go off separately and do it to the best of their ability. That way they won't distract from the rest of the group. This also helps you identify who is on board with the larger initiative.

Step 2. Educate the Task Force

You can't just let the group "happen." You have to intentionally educate stakeholders to

- understand the determinants of heavy drinking
- understand the concentric circles model
- recognize that environmental factors (such as alcohol availability) are the keys to intervention for the majority of binge drinkers

Without this educational effort, your stakeholders will lack a common understanding of the problem. Each stakeholder brings a personal perspective and bias. The job of the steering group is to try to fit the diverse collection of perspectives your stakeholders bring to the table within the larger umbrella of interventions that are known to change the drinking environment of the campus. A public health perspective is unique; it can effectively encompass a wide range of perspectives, while at the same time keep the group focused on solutions that can work.

It is important to focus attention on changing the environment to reduce the frequency of binge drinking and the severity of consequences. In our research, schools that focused only on individual interventions remained the same or even lost ground in solving their binge-drinking problem. On the other hand, schools that included environmental initiatives had success at reducing the patterns of binge drinking.[31]

Stakeholders may be unfamiliar with the idea of addressing binge drinking as a public health challenge and discouraged by the sense that the most impactful environmental interventions feel beyond the reach of any individual stakeholder's purview. The steering group needs to keep this in mind. It should encourage stakeholders to tackle the small things that they can control (and want to do) while aligning those with the larger task of changing the environment that ultimately facilitates binge drinking.

The steering committee should seek to shape the overall flow of interventions to align with the environmental approach and the changes that members know will work for their campus. But it also should allow everyone to act on his or her favored solutions while reminding all stakeholders of the bigger picture.

Experience has shown that groups can get bogged down fighting over the "right" solutions to binge drinking on campus. This internal battle can quickly derail the group. Though the group will have to sort through priorities, arguments over the best approach are usually fruitless. It is far more important that the steering group keep everyone moving forward in the same general direction. Allow individual stakeholders to pursue the goals that they feel will work, as long as they are generally in the right direction. This approach keeps the group motivated while building cohesion around what works. It also defuses the tendency to struggle over "best" solutions. Using this approach, you can encourage a variety of interventions that can coexist. Some will be more effective than others. Your job is to spend as little time as possible on unproven or ineffective ones, encourage and lead the ones that align with the truly effective strategies, maintain enthusiasm, and use the data you collect to shift people toward more effective tactics.

Administrative stakeholders' jobs are to help and support individual students and make college a positive experience. The public health approach to binge drinking requires a variety of environmental strategies that shape the behavior of students as a *group,* as well as interventions that help students as *individuals.* Unfortunately, the public health approach is sometimes perceived as being all about punishments and sanctions. In reality it is primarily about promoting community standards about the availability of alcohol (which sometimes involves sanctions). The public health/environmental approach has been effective in changing more lives in many arenas, and the evidence shows it is an effective approach for alcohol as well.

This is why educating stakeholders about what works is a key job of the steering committee. Past efforts have been undermined when the coalition was not on the same page. A concerted effort to educate your members can help avoid those problems. Here's what the stakeholder education should emphasize:

- Be sure stakeholders understand the nature of the problem as a public health issue. Gather and present data on the scope of the problem, the impact on students individually and as a group, and the impact on the surrounding community.

- Explain how the environmentally focused solutions work. Show and explain how the research data support these solutions.

- Encourage the members to avoid jumping to problem resolution immediately. Jumping to solutions is very typical, but in fact the stakeholder group needs to gather data and understand the nature and scope of the problems and known resolutions before discussing possible resolutions.

- If the stakeholder group has been together for some time, members need to do an honest assessment of whether and to what degree the things they've been doing have worked. Compare those successes and failures to the information in this book. The group may need to take time to decide how to push the "reset" button on its work, so it can step back and think carefully about the solutions it has been attempting.

- Remind the group, whether new or existing, that the environmental conditions that give rise to binge drinking did not develop overnight. Solutions can and should be long term. The group does not need to rush to succeed. The changes necessary will take time.

Two brief articles may help educate your team: Widening the Lens, Sharpening the Focus and The Prevention Paradox and a Public Health Approach to Student Drinking.[32]

Step 3. Assess Group Capacity

Even if your group has been together for years, we suggest that you pause and assess the current and available resources, skills, and perspectives of the people on the task force and the programs, data, processes, and services on campus.

A warning, though, before you get started: there can be a tendency among groups, especially on campuses, to assess forever without taking action. Use assessment to advance your strategic efforts. The group should turn its efforts to assessing the conditions and resources in the following areas:

- people, skills, and time availability
- financial resources
- preferences

What follows is a partial list of what you might assess in each area. A thorough, formal assessment may not be necessary, but an awareness of your group's capacity will be helpful later when you need to draw on those resources to create real change. We provide examples of how you should explore each category.

People, Skills, and Time Availability

- What is our current membership? Are people attending regularly?
- Do we have members who are skilled at handling the logistics, such as meeting minutes, reminders, setting agendas, tracking expenditures, and monitoring progress?
- What data collection and analysis tools do we have access to? Who in our group is good at data collection, analysis, and interpretation?
- Who has been engaged previously? Who hasn't been invited but should be?

- What skills does each current member bring?
- Do we have enough people who can spare the time to commit to our plans?
- What skills do we need, given what we know about the particular alcohol issues facing our campus? For example, do we need people with expertise in data collection, analysis, and interpretation? community organizing? issue advocacy? message development and dissemination? fundraising?

As you assess your people resources, consider at least five potential roles for task force members:

1. Providing direct services, such as working with students via health care, housing, student affairs, or campus and community security and law enforcement
2. Performing administrative, strategic, or management tasks
3. Developing and writing policy; working with others to ensure that policy is implemented
4. Engaging in public relations activity
5. Community organizing

Members may fill more than one role, but they should fill at least one of the roles. There should be some balance. For example, you can't have a task force composed of only people in direct service provision.

One activity for leadership is to develop a list of roles that each member can play and make sure that each person is making a positive contribution to one or more of these areas. Also make sure that there are enough people who can perform in each of these roles. Gaps in one or more areas mean that the group is unbalanced and you need to recruit or develop talent in that area. (The exercise Assessing Representation in step 1 may help you determine gaps in team membership.) The identification of the roles each member plays can assist with mapping out strategy. Such identification ensures that you have the ability and the right people involved to execute the strategies and tactics you develop. (Part of the reason some strategies do not get implemented is that the group does not have the right people deployed to make them happen.)

If the skills you have don't match what you need, you can often find the needed skills on campus. Most stakeholder groups do not include people from the political science, statistics, business, marketing, media, or anthropology departments, and yet the skills those people possess can be profoundly useful when trying to change an environment that leads to binge drinking.

The binge-drinking problem is a community phenomenon, not just a campus problem. Therefore, you should also turn to people from the community who carry the requisite skills.

Many print and online resources can supplement the skills of your group. For example, the American Medical Association has material on media advocacy regarding alcohol issues on its website. Many organizations provide support in coalition development, community organizing, legislative advocacy, and so forth. As you identify what you need, the sources to fill those gaps will become evident. If members of your coalition or task force don't have these skills, invest in talented, committed people and get them appropriate training. These skills will be invaluable for executing a strategy to enact the types of interventions that work.[33]

Be sure to identify individuals within the group who can be effective advocates to the community. Your efforts amount to a political campaign. Get the right message and talking points together, and train stakeholders in using them. Opportunities to advocate for your goals can present themselves at surprising times, so you need to be prepared to act when the opportunity arrives.

Financial Resources

- What are our current sources of funds?
- Are our sources sustainable into the future?
- Are we using the funds we have effectively?

- Do we have a diverse funding base?
- Are we accepting money or in-kind support from the alcohol industry? (If so, see the case example How the Alcohol Industry Derails Alcohol Prevention on page 179.)
- Have we developed clear policies for the acceptance, rejection, allocation, and tracking of funds?
- What types of in-kind and cash-equivalent resources are we prepared to accept?
- Do we have the skills and permission to raise funds, and do we have the proper support to track funds?

Group Preferences

Finally, we encourage you to assess the current baseline of preferences regarding alcohol intervention tactics. You can do this informally by talking to your membership, or more formally by asking members to complete a survey. Document 2 on the CD-ROM contains questions we have used in the evaluation of the AMOD (A Matter of Degree) program. You may use any or all of these questions when you survey your coalition membership. The data you obtain can reveal what your group feels about your activities, identify gaps in support for various interventions that inform your strategic planning, and provide information to track progress within your task force over time. These questions can be easily programmed into one of many free or low-cost survey tools.

If there is a lack of support in your coalition for working on the strategies recommended in this book, you will need to work to develop support among key members or recruit members who will support those initiatives. Forging ahead if your group is not supportive will create problems later on. In our opinion, a lack of support for strategies that work at the outset is a major reason that a college will have little progress in reducing student drinking. Take the time to talk to key people about why you want to pursue the strategies that work.

As a result of step 3, you'll have a clear understanding of the group's skills and preferences. You'll know what kinds of finances, programs, and processes you have in place, and you'll understand the connections among them. The next step is to get a clear picture of the alcohol environment on campus and in the surrounding community.

Step 4. Assess the Alcohol Environment

As you work to change the conditions that facilitate binge drinking on campus, you need to know where you've started—otherwise you won't be able to judge your progress. This involves an assessment of *indicator data* about the alcohol environment.

Document 3 on the CD-ROM can help you assess indicator information in depth. Program Evaluation Guide to the Collection of Campus and Community Indicators was originally developed for the Harvard School of Public Health evaluation of the AMOD (A Matter of Degree) program. Collecting the information recommended in this guide will help you to understand the campus and community context in which student drinking occurs, identify areas where you can make improvements, and establish baseline measures to track improvement. We encourage you to collect these data at the outset of your efforts. This information will be invaluable to your group when advocating for policy change and increased resources.

We suggest the following areas for gathering data:

- alcohol use, student surveys, and indicator data (arrests, complaints, and so forth)
- alcohol access on and near campus

Data on Use Patterns and Consequences

The stakeholder group needs direct data on student alcohol use, more general data from student surveys, and indicator data on arrests, complaints, and so forth. It will also need data on the impact of its activities over time. Some questions for your assessment:

- What information is available through campus student surveys? Most campuses have student survey information available. If not, several organizations specialize in data collection with college students. One such survey research organization we have worked with is Survey Sciences Group in Ann Arbor, Michigan. For a modest fee, this organization can provide high-quality data about your student population. Numerous banks of survey questions are available to guide the development of a survey questionnaire. We recommend asking questions that are consistent with the questions asked in large national surveys so that you can compare your campus results. These include the National Household Survey on Drug Abuse, the National Epidemiologic Survey on Alcohol and Related Conditions (NESARC), the University of Michigan Monitoring the Future Study, and the Centers for Disease Control and Prevention Behavioral Risk Factor Surveillance System.
- What indicator data do we have or need access to? Indicator data include records of arrests, citations, complaints, internal referrals for counseling or discipline, reports on use at local retail establishments, and so forth.
- Are our sources of data reliable and consistent?
- What indicators will we track over time to understand if we have had an impact on the problem? Do we have valid and reliable baseline data for those indicators from prior years?

For example, there is reasonable evidence that student alcohol use follows seasonal or event-driven patterns. Indicator data such as arrests often spike at the beginning of the school year, during homecoming, and at Halloween, and plummet during finals week. Armed with that data, you can actively track these linkages and then undertake event-specific interventions.

Alcohol Access

You need to be aware of the availability of alcohol on and near campus. Develop a community map that shows retail sources to which students have ready access.

- What are the retail alcohol outlets within easy access of campus?
- What are the target markets and pricing strategies of those outlets? That is, do they clearly target young people, offer deep discounts on special days, and so forth?
- What community and campus regulations affect distribution and consumption of alcohol?
- What student housing, on and off campus, has a reputation for heavy drinking and related problems?
- What seasonal or event-related activities change the accessibility of alcohol in the neighborhood? (For example, alcohol may be available at special events like Oktoberfest or Springfest, downtown days, game days, and so forth.)

A physical map can help you spot trends and suggest ways to reduce access. Discussions with the local police can help the group learn which bars appeal to young people and which bar owners are more likely to support the stakeholder group's aims. Working with police to map data on calls and citations can help focus local efforts, and also serve as a useful tool when advocating for policy changes.

Helpful Data Tools

Here are some tools that can support your data collection.

Public Opinion Survey of Leaders and People in the Community

Public opinion surveys can be used to set a strategic agenda and advocate for the policies that will move your community in the right direction, to identify concerns about drinking issues and potential support for given strategies, and to support your efforts to influence decision makers. (For sample questions, see document 4 on the CD-ROM, Sample Public

Opinion Survey Questions.)[34] You can find ideas for additional questions and an example of a report write-up at the following website: www.epi.umn.edu/alcohol/pubopin/index.shtm.

The Internet makes surveying easy and affordable. Many universities have their own capacity to survey students, faculty, staff, and people living in the community (usually found within the college office of institutional research). If not, it is possible to use one of many free or low-cost services for conducting surveys.

Campus and Community Policies

In addition to collecting information about public opinion on student alcohol use, it is important to collect information on the policies about alcohol that exist on campus (including within organizations on campus), as well as local community or state alcohol policies.

Alcohol policies in your state are available from the National Institute on Alcohol Abuse and Alcoholism Alcohol Policy Information System at www.alcoholpolicy.niaaa.nih.gov. Here, you can see how your state compares with others and identify areas that may need tightening.

Alcohol policies on campus may be collected by contacting the relevant departments (student health services, housing, etc.).

Community Alcohol Outlets and Alcohol Incident Reports

Create a map of community alcohol outlets, which can be very useful in understanding how to change access. Many sophisticated software applications can do mapping work, and you may have expertise in doing this on your campus. Advances in websites such as Google Maps or Bing now make it possible for you to create your own maps and identify where these establishments are located and what they are close to (e.g., schools, day care centers, churches, and so forth). You can also link these maps to police incident data to look at the relationship between alcohol access and crime hotspots. These types of maps have proved effective in advocacy efforts to reduce access to alcohol.

Beyond these important pieces of data, a wide range of existing data can provide you with information about the nature of alcohol use on your campus and in your local community. As previously noted, the Program Evaluation Guide to the Collection of Campus and Community Indicators (document 3) identifies sources of data and provides guidance on how to collect information for use in advocacy and outcome monitoring.

Sustaining the Task Force

As the task force moves from internal examination and capacity building to implementation, it needs to keep itself motivated and sustain its efforts over the long haul. Here are three keys to the sustainability of the task force.

Have a Plan

The task force should develop a formal, detailed plan as to how the task force itself, and its programs and services, can be sustained. At minimum, the plan needs to address

- the group's long-term governance, including how membership and leadership structure is to be maintained and refreshed

- funding for programs

- supporting the integration of task force programs into the college's student health system

Evaluate Programs and Practices

The sustainability of the task force can be strengthened by evidence of the success of the programs and practices. It

continued on next page

can be expensive and impractical to conduct controlled and scientifically rigorous program evaluations. But ongoing data collection and even anecdotal or case study evidence and reports, as well as process evaluation data (e.g., how many students are served), can be valuable. Universities with programs of study in evaluation can recruit skilled students for this work.

Engage Individual Members in Meaningful Ways

A sustainable task force places a high priority on implementing strategies that promote stakeholder *engagement.* Engagement by task force members can be enhanced in several ways:

- ▶ the person's role and involvement is perceived by the person as meaningful to the task force

- ▶ the commitment and burden associated with participation is not viewed as excessive

- ▶ the goals and activities of the task force are perceived by the member as relevant, practical, and effective

- ▶ "external" barriers to involvement are minimal (e.g., favorable schedule of task force meetings; support by the member's supervisor or boss)

- ▶ relationships are built and maintained among task force members and related stakeholders on campus and with the local community

- ▶ the task force and its programs are highly visible (e.g., public relations campaigns; hosting events that celebrate program milestones)

Step 5. Begin Implementation

The assessment of group capacity and alcohol use patterns can feel overwhelming, but it needn't be perfect. Go far enough to understand the key areas that will inform your work into the future; you can always continue to uncover new information. The greatest resource gap is typically not even money but time, skills, and commitment. You need to find the right people with the right skills who have a passion for changing the campus environment to protect students from the problems associated with binge drinking.

A key benefit of the analysis of the resources and gaps will help you identify ways to shift the responsibilities of some stakeholders, freeing up their time for actions that better fit their positions. For example, a dean who spends ten hours per week meeting with students to talk about alcohol issues and bad behavior may make better use of his or her time and positional authority to be in contact with key constituents—alumni, city councilors, and so forth—who can help to change the environment.

Implementation involves developing a plan to take action on each of the five strategies outlined at the beginning of this chapter. As a reminder, those strategies were

Strategy 1: Implement a screening and intervention system on campus to identify and help students who experience problems related to their drinking.

Strategy 2: Improve campus policies and procedures for addressing student alcohol issues.

Strategy 3: Limit the availability of alcohol by reducing marketing, reducing outlet density, and improving responsible beverage service standards.

Strategy 4: Enforce existing policies on underage drinking, service to intoxicated patrons, and alcohol-impaired driving.

Strategy 5: Increase the price of alcohol through taxes and by eliminating price discounting.

The next chapters discuss aspects of these strategies. *Before* developing an implementation plan, you will need to review those chapters and discuss the strategies in the context of your campus situation, the group's capacities and preferences, your financial resources, and other factors unique to your situation. However, the following tips will help you as you implement strategies:

- Don't waste time looking for a magic bullet. Choose several strategies that are consistent with a public health perspective and begin pursing them.
- Don't waste time arguing about which practices are best. This saps energy from the task force. If there is conflict, often several strategies can be pursued at the same time. Just try to work on each of them efficiently.
- Identify where you think you'll have early success, achieve it, and build on that.
- Create a list of milestone indicators that will show movement toward goals and track movement.
- Keep the group apprised of successes using a regular status update.
- Help the group members hold each other accountable for commitments they've made.
- Find and use public relations opportunities. Keep your communications strategic and consistent.

Chapter Summary

In this chapter, you learned about the five strategies recommended for addressing binge drinking on campus. You've developed a steering group and assembled a task force (or tweaked an existing one). You've assessed the group's capacities and the alcohol environment. And you've begun work toward implementation. In the next chapter, you'll learn about what to include in your campus screening and intervention system.

CHAPTER 4

IMPLEMENTING A SCREENING
AND INTERVENTION SYSTEM

The student health system on campuses can play a significant role in addressing students' problem drinking. Services pertaining to screening, referral, and, if possible, intervention and treatment should be included in all comprehensive efforts to reduce underage drinking. We appreciate that barriers exist in implementing clinical services, such as lack of staff for addressing alcohol problems and poor support from college and university administrators. However, awareness about convenient and research-based services can help mitigate barriers. In this chapter, we review the two primary clinical services—screening and interventions—which now benefit from a strong research base. These services are in the purview of most college student health systems.

Screening

A campus health service system must have formal procedures in place to actively screen and identify those students in need of help for alcohol-related problems. Screening is a critical step toward identifying students who are abusing alcohol and may need intervention or treatment services. The goal of screening is to briefly and efficiently evaluate a person to determine if he or she needs a more comprehensive clinical assessment. Thus, a screening procedure provides a probable picture as to whether or not the individual has a problem. If the screening procedure suggests that a problem exists, the next step is for the individual to receive a comprehensive assessment in which the evaluation focuses on the presence or absence of a formal diagnosis and the need for treatment. Table 4.1 summarizes the distinguishing features of screening and comprehensive assessment procedures.

TABLE 4.1

Features That Distinguish between a Screening and Comprehensive Assessment

TASK	HOW TASK WILL ASSIST WITH IDENTIFICATION OF A DRINKING PROBLEM	REFERRAL DECISION
Screening	Does the student *probably* have a drinking problem or not?	If there are positive indications of a drinking problem, refer the student for a comprehensive assessment.
Comprehensive Assessment	Does the student *likely* have a drinking problem or not?	If there are definitive indications of a drinking problem, refer the student for an intervention or intensive treatment.

Whom to Screen?

Given the relatively high prevalence rate of alcohol problems among college students, some level of screening of alcohol problems should occur during routine visits at campus health care clinics. Also, screening expertise can be extended to a wider net of individuals who are likely to come in contact with alcohol-impaired students. These individuals include the following:

- residence hall staff
- educational counseling staff
- campus security staff
- athletic training staff
- law enforcement agents

Screening Procedures

Fortunately, there are several user-friendly and scientifically sound screening instruments for use with college students suspected of having a drinking problem. A recent study on this topic reviewed the group of standardized alcohol screening tools and judged that five of them are suitable for use with college students.[35] These five favorable tools are brief, valid, and reliable and provide useful ways to capture the relative frequency of personal and social consequences of drinking in college-age young people. Also, all of them are in the public domain and thus are free. (As a side note, this study found that 44 percent of the surveyed college health officials reported their school used an available and standardized screening tool, yet only about half of these schools used one of the preferred tools.)

Table 4.2 contains a summary (with our comments) of the five exemplary tools for screening college students for alcohol problems identified in the study referenced above. These tools are in the public domain and were chosen based on their favorable psychometric properties when used with college students. Document 5: Screening Tools provides a copy of each screening instrument.

TABLE 4.2

Select Alcohol Abuse Screening Instruments for College Students[36]

INSTRUMENT	SOURCE REFERENCE	NUMBER OF ITEMS	DESCRIPTION	COMMENTS
AUDIT (Alcohol Use Disorders Test)	Babor, T. F. et al. (2001). *AUDIT: The Alcohol Use Disorders Identification Test: Guidelines for Use in Primary Care.* Geneva, Switzerland: World Health Organization.	10	Ten-item alcohol screening questionnaire with three questions on the amount and frequency of drinking, three questions on alcohol dependence, and four on problems caused by alcohol. A range of scores have been shown to be accurate in identifying a problem drinker. An optimal cutoff score of 6 has been recommended for college students.[37]	Perhaps the gold standard of screening measures for alcohol problems.
College Alcohol Problem Scale– Revised (CAPS-r)	O'Hare, T. (1997). Measuring problem drinking in first-time offenders: Development and validation of the College Alcohol Problem Scale (CAPS). *Journal of Substance Abuse Treatment,* 14: 383–87.	8	This eight-item self-report scale measures the frequency of personal and social problems associated with drinking in college students.	Provides a focus on psychosocial consequences associated with heavy drinking.

continued on next page

TABLE 4.2

Select Alcohol Abuse Screening Instruments
for College Students[36]

INSTRUMENT	SOURCE REFERENCE	NUMBER OF ITEMS	DESCRIPTION	COMMENTS
CRAFFT	Knight, J. R. et al. (2002). Validity of the CRAFFT substance abuse screening test among adolescent clinic patients. *Archives of Pediatric Adolescent Medicine,* 156: 607–14.	6	This tool consists of six yes/no mnemonic items (e.g., the R represents the item "Do you ever use alcohol or drugs to RELAX, feel better about yourself, or fit in?"). Two or more endorsements (yes responses) is highly predictive of an alcohol problem.	Best used for younger college students, given that most of its psychometric data pertain to adolescents.
CUGE	Aertgeerts, B. et al. (2000). The value of CAGE, CUGE, and AUDIT in screening for alcohol abuse and dependence among college freshmen. *Alcoholism: Clinical and Experimental Research,* 24: 53–57.	4	The CUGE consists of four yes/no mnemonic items (e.g., C = cut down; U = under influence; G = guilty feelings; E = eye opener). A cutoff score of 1 or more is predictive of an alcohol problem.	A solid brief screen.

continued on next page

TABLE 4.2

Select Alcohol Abuse Screening Instruments for College Students[36]

INSTRUMENT	SOURCE REFERENCE	NUMBER OF ITEMS	DESCRIPTION	COMMENTS
Rapid Alcohol Problems Screen (RAPS4)	Cherpitel, C. J. (2000). A brief screening instrument for alcohol dependence in the emergency room: The RAPS4. *Journal of Studies on Alcohol*, 61: 447–49.	4	The RAPS4 is a four-item instrument that provides high sensitivity and specificity for recent (prior year) alcohol dependence. A positive response to any one of the items signifies positive for an alcohol dependence disorder as defined by DSM-IV criteria.	Excellent choice to help gauge if a student's drinking may have progressed to alcohol dependence.

Comprehensive Assessment

In an ideal situation, a student who has an elevated score on a screening tool (as determined by the scoring rule for the screening tool) should then be administered an additional and more comprehensive assessment. Of course, this translates to more burden on the student health program in terms of staff time and cost. For colleges with minimal resources, the responsible action for the person doing the screening is to recommend that the student receive a comprehensive assessment at a community-based mental health clinic or drug treatment program. For colleges with the capabilities of conducting in-house assessments, there are numerous standardized, comprehensive interviews to guide this process. Table 4.3 summarizes a group of well-known and validated interviews (with our comments) that are suitable for college students, and document 6 provides a more detailed description of each. All of these tools assist in problem identification, referral decisions, and treatment planning. Selection may depend on length (some are rather lengthy), cost (not all are public domain), and training requirements (some require training). But the good news is that an assessor has psychometrically sound tools to assist with a comprehensive assessment.

TABLE 4.3

Clinical Interviews for a Comprehensive Assessment[38]

INSTRUMENT	SOURCE REFERENCE	TIME (MIN.)	TRAINING NEEDED	SCORING TIME (MIN.)	COMPUTER SCORING	FEE FOR USE	COMMENTS
Adolescent Diagnostic Interview (ADI)	Winters, K. C. et al. (1993). Assessing alcohol and cannabis use disorders in an adolescent clinical sample. *Psychology of Addictive Behaviors, 7:* 185–96.	45–55	No	15	No	No	Highly structured interview, with a primary focus on drug use history and DSM-IV criteria for substance use disorders.
Comprehensive Adolescent Severity Inventory (CASI-A)	Meyers, K. et al. (1995). The development of the Comprehensive Addiction Severity Index for Adolescents (CASI-A): An interview for assessing multiple problems of adolescents. *Journal of Substance Abuse Treatment, 12:* 181–93.	45–90	Yes	15	Yes	Yes (computer version)	Semi-structured interview with excellent coverage of the person's psychosocial functioning. It includes assessment of DSM-IV substance use disorders.

continued on next page

TABLE 4.3

Clinical Interviews for a Comprehensive Assessment[38]

INSTRUMENT	SOURCE REFERENCE	TIME (MIN.)	TRAINING NEEDED	SCORING TIME (MIN.)	COMPUTER SCORING	FEE FOR USE	COMMENTS
Global Appraisal of Individual Needs (GAIN)	Dennis, M. L. (1999). *Global Appraisal of Individual Needs (GAIN): Administration Guide for the GAIN and Related Measures.* Bloomington, IL: Lighthouse Publications.	60–120	Yes	15	Yes	Yes	A semi-structured interview that has been heavily researched. It has in-depth coverage of the person's functioning in multiple life areas. It includes assessment of DSM-IV substance use disorders.
Teen Addiction Severity Index (T-ASI)	Kaminer, Y. et al. (1991). The Teen Addiction Severity Index (T-ASI): Rationale and reliability. *International Journal of the Addictions,* 26: 219–26.	20–45	Yes	10	No	No	Semi-structured interview with excellent coverage of DSM-IV criteria for substance use disorders and psychosocial functioning.

Intervention Services

It is estimated that approximately 20 percent of college students may need some type of intervention or treatment for their alcohol use,[39] and most of these students do not recognize the need for help. For example, a longitudinal study of college students' health behaviors[40] that tracked 1,253 undergraduates at a large public college found that only 3.6 percent of students that met criteria for a substance use disorder (the most prevalent being an alcohol use disorder) perceived a need for professional help. When a student receives treatment, it is most likely following an alcohol-related legal incident rather than seeking treatment voluntarily.[41] Many of the four-year colleges in the United States do not offer the evidence-based alcohol intervention programs that are recommended by the National Institute on Alcohol Abuse and Alcoholism[42] and most colleges do not offer alcohol treatment services.[43] This large gap in available services runs counter to the fact that an extensive body of research has emerged in the past twenty years examining the benefits of various types of interventions to reduce heavy drinking among college students. This literature includes several *qualitative* scholarly reviews of the literature—the most prominent include the two comprehensive reviews by Mary Larimer and Jessica Cronce[44]—and select reviews of particular types of interventions: feedback-based interventions;[45] individual-level interventions;[46] and computer-administered programs.[47] Also, a *quantitative* meta-analysis of the research has been conducted[48] because of the large number of published controlled studies.

The following quote from the Kate Carey et al. meta-analysis best sums up this body of work: "In sum, providing interventions to reduce hazardous drinking by college students is clearly worthwhile. These results demonstrate that risk reduction interventions for college drinkers result in significantly less drinking over follow-up intervals lasting up to 6 months" (p. 2489).

Of course, this book is oriented toward a multidimensional approach. Thus, we contend that the benefits from clinically oriented interventions would be enhanced by establishing systems for consistently screening and providing intervention services that reach as many students as possible and supplementing them with environmental changes, such as coordinated media, policy, law enforcement, and community initiatives.

The integration of multiple components offers the greatest promise of reducing drinking by college students.

Synthesis of Findings

Based on our synthesis of the various literature reviews and the meta-analysis noted above, we have identified four summary themes, after which we list select intervention programs that are supported by the research literature.

1. Cognitive-behavioral Therapy and Motivational Enhancement

The research comparing intervention versus control conditions indicates that the greatest intervention benefits are produced with cognitive-behavioral therapy (CBT) or motivational enhancement (ME) approaches—and when these approaches incorporate a personalized normative feedback component. The benefits include reducing alcohol use and alcohol-related problems. However, the contrast between students who receive interventions and those in control conditions diminishes over time.

CBT aims to solve a student's problems of dysfunctional emotions, behaviors, and cognitions through goal-oriented, systematic procedures. Common CBT approaches used in the addiction field include cognitive correction, problem-solving training, social skills training, and relapse prevention. ME refers to a therapy approach that assumes the individual has or can acquire the knowledge and skills to make behavior change, and seeks primarily to enhance motivation to change.[49] Elements of effective ME include objective and nonjudgmental feedback, enhancement of personal responsibility for change, direct advice, a menu of options for change, an empathic therapeutic interviewing style, and the support of self-accomplishment. It is common for a counselor to combine these two approaches when conducting a brief intervention. Both share the common elements of negotiating with the individual to identify realistic and obtainable goals, and to strengthen the individual's skills toward obtaining the goals.

The research also highlights the importance of brief intervention for heavy drinkers to include this additional component: personalized normative feedback (PNF). PNF uses information designed to correct normative misperceptions to reduce heavy drinking. Information about a student's *own* drinking levels and the student's *perception of others'* drinking levels are compared to normative information about others' actual drinking. The discrepancies provided by this comparison are designed to change the student's perceptions of what is normal drinking, and thus change his or her drinking levels to a safer level.

2. Individual, Face-to-face Interventions

Individual, face-to-face interventions, as opposed to group interventions, appear to be the most effective mode of delivery, although there is some support for providing personalized normative feedback with a mailing or computerized approach.

Individual-based interventions have shown greater benefits as compared to delivering these techniques in a group setting. This may be due to the high level of personalization that can occur when counseling is delivered on an individual basis. A mailing or computerized approach, with its moderate ability to deliver therapeutic ingredients in a personalized way, may not be optimal from an outcome-effectiveness standpoint. However, these approaches provide a cost-effective alternative with an expectation of moderate benefits when face-to-face counseling is not an option.

3. Personalized Normative Feedback Approach

There is mixed or no support found for the personalized normative feedback approach when it is used as the only strategy (as noted above). This approach is based on research that suggests that college students often overestimate the amount of alcohol consumed by fellow students. It is believed such misperceptions of normative drinking behavior lead some students to consume more alcohol in an effort to reflect what they perceive to be normal group behavior. This strategy informs students of the true norms for alcohol consumption on their campus.

4. Interventions with Mandated Students

There is emerging evidence for the effectiveness of interventions with mandated students (students who are ordered to attend an intervention). Two of the major literature reviews noted above addressed mandated programs[50] and they both concluded that support exists for the use of evidenced-based interventions for mandated college students. One caution: most of these studies used an active comparison group rather than a wait-list control group, given the ethical dilemma of a wait-list condition with mandated students. Thus, it is difficult to attribute the reductions in alcohol use to intervention effects because the sanction itself may also have influenced the beneficial changes.

Select Evidence-based Interventions for College Students

The summary of this literature indicates that binge-drinking interventions for college students often consist of at least one of two therapeutic components. One component is cognitive-behavioral skills training. This approach seeks to change the student's beliefs and thinking about the use of alcohol via activities such as altering expectancies about alcohol's effects, educating the student about normative drinking levels among other students, documenting daily alcohol consumption, and learning how to better manage stress. The second core component is the use of motivational enhancement interviewing techniques. As the term implies, motivational enhancement is a counseling style designed to stimulate students' intrinsic desire or motivation to change their behaviors.

Table 4.4 summarizes evidence-based intervention programs and practices for use with college students identified as having a drinking problem. Inclusion of a program in the table required that the program or approach (a) was rigorously evaluated and results were published in at least one peer-reviewed publication, (b) showed significant reductions in alcohol involvement at follow-up, and (c) in instances where the study design permitted, outperformed a control condition (e.g., waiting list, assessment only).

TABLE 4.4

Evidenced-based Programs[51]

PROGRAM OR APPROACH	SOURCE REFERENCES	DESCRIPTION
Alcohol 101 Plus CD-ROM	Donohue, B. et al. (2004). A controlled evaluation of two prevention programs in reducing alcohol use among college students at low and high risk for alcohol-related problems. *Journal of Alcohol and Drug Education,* 48: 13–33.	This 45-minute psycho-educational prevention program consists of an interactive CD-ROM in which students respond to computer icons that are relevant to alcohol use, including attendance at a "virtual party" where they make choices for video characters placed in social situations involving alcohol and positive and negative consequences. Participants may also visit a "virtual bar" that provides information on their estimated blood alcohol concentration based on number of drinks consumed, weight, and other relevant factors. Other icons lead to information about alcohol refusal skills, consequences of unsafe sex and underage drinking, comparisons of participant drinking rates with college norm rates, multiple-choice games relevant to alcohol, and depictions of real-life campus tragedies involving alcohol misuse.

continued on next page

TABLE 4.4

Evidenced-based Programs[51]

PROGRAM OR APPROACH	SOURCE REFERENCES	DESCRIPTION
AlcoholEdu for College	Paschall, M. J. et al. (2011). Effects of AlcoholEdu for College on alcohol-related problems among freshmen: A randomized multicampus trial. *Journal of Studies on Alcohol and Drugs,* 72: 642–50. Paschall, M. J. et al. (2011). Evaluation of an Internet-based alcohol misuse prevention course for college freshmen: Findings of a randomized multi-campus trial. *American Journal of Preventive Medicine,* 41: 300–308.	AlcoholEdu for College is a two- to three-hour online alcohol prevention program designed to impact both students and campus culture. Thus, the program aims to reduce individual and institutional risks associated with alcohol abuse. It is designed to be given to an entire population of students, such as an entering first-year class. This method creates a learning experience that seeks to motivate behavior change, reset unrealistic expectations about the effects of alcohol, link choices about drinking to academic and personal success, and promote student health and campus safety.

continued on next page

TABLE 4.4

Evidenced-based Programs[51]

PROGRAM OR APPROACH	SOURCE REFERENCES	DESCRIPTION
Brief Alcohol Screening and Intervention for College Students (BASICS) and Webversion, mystudent body.com	Borsari, B. and Carey, K. B. (2005). Two brief alcohol interventions for mandated college students. *Psychology of Addictive Behaviors,* 19: 296–302. Chiauzzi, E. et al. (2005). My Student Body: A high-risk drinking prevention website for college students. *Journal of American College Health,* 53: 263–74. Dimeff, L. A. et al. (1999). *Brief Alcohol Screening and Intervention for College Students.* New York: Guilford Press. Marlatt, G.A. et al. (1998). Screening and brief intervention for high-risk college student drinkers: Results from a 2-year follow-up assessment. *Journal of Consulting and Clinical Psychology,* 66: 604–15.	Following a harm-reduction approach and using motivational interviewing techniques, BASICS aims to motivate students to reduce alcohol use in order to decrease the negative consequences of drinking. It is delivered over the course of two one-hour interviews with a brief online assessment survey taken by the student after the first session. The first interview gathers information about the student's recent alcohol consumption patterns, personal beliefs about alcohol, and drinking history. Information from the online assessment survey is used to develop a customized feedback profile for use in the second interview, which compares personal alcohol use with alcohol use norms, reviews individualized negative consequences and risk factors, clarifies perceived risks and benefits of drinking, and provides options to assist in making changes to decrease or abstain from alcohol use.

continued on next page

TABLE 4.4

Evidenced-based Programs[51]

PROGRAM OR APPROACH	SOURCE REFERENCES	DESCRIPTION
Brief Alcohol Screening and Intervention for College Students (BASICS) and Webversion, mystudent body.com		A Web version of BASICS was developed by Chiauzzi and colleagues. Mystudentbody.com is an online, subscription-based program that uses the same personalized motivational feed-back approach to persuade a college student to reduce alcohol use and the risk factors associated with use. Implementation of the program requires that an on-campus program administrator receive training to learn how to customize the program for the college and to be able to respond to students' questions. The program also includes a parent component, which admin-istrators can offer to families to provide them with resources for discussing sensitive topics and helping students make a healthy transition to college life.

continued on next page

TABLE 4.4

Evidenced-based Programs[51]

PROGRAM OR APPROACH	SOURCE REFERENCES	DESCRIPTION
Brief Motivational Interviewing (BMI)	Miller, W. R. and Rollnick, S. (2002). *Motivational Interviewing: Preparing People for Change* (2nd ed.). New York: Guilford Press.	The development of BMI was based on three core assumptions: (1) the individual is ambivalent about the need to change drinking behavior; (2) risk or harm reduction is more acceptable to the person than abstinence; and (3) students have the motivation and the skills to use drinking reduction strategies. A common strategy of this approach is to assess the student's drinking patterns in order to construct a personal drinking profile (e.g., quantity-frequency consumed, peak blood alcohol level, amount of money spent on alcohol, caloric intake) and then engage the student in a normative comparison exercise (e.g., beliefs about peers' drinking; amount consumed in relation to peers). Another common technique of BMI is the decisional balance (DB) exercise. This activity aims at revealing the discrepancy between the student's risky drinking behavior and his or her goals and values.

continued on next page

TABLE 4.4

Evidenced-based Programs[51]

PROGRAM OR APPROACH	SOURCE REFERENCES	DESCRIPTION
e-CHECK-UP TO GO	Walters, S. T. et al. (2007). A controlled trial of Web-based feedback for heavy-drinking college students. *Prevention Science*, 8: 83–88.	The e-CHECKUP TO GO program (informally known as *e-CHUG*) is a personalized, evidence-based, online prevention intervention that has separate curriculum to address alcohol and marijuana use. Based on motivational interviewing and social norms theory, this program is designed to motivate individuals to reduce their consumption using personalized information about their own substance use and risk factors associated with use. Each basic program is self-guided and takes about 20–30 minutes to complete. Also, the student can complete a *personal checkup* on multiple occasions to track changes about his or her use and risk behaviors. If a counselor wishes to use the program in conjunction with face-to-face contact, the student can be asked to complete the companion *Personal Reflections* program. This feature requires an additional 15–20 minutes and asks students to respond to questions designed to further examine their personal choices and the social norms surrounding and influencing their use of substances.

Chapter Summary

It behooves colleges to implement screening and intervention services for their students. The relatively high prevalence of problem drinking among college students and the availability of both scientifically sound and user-friendly screening tools and intervention programs add up to compelling reasons for colleges to adopt and offer these clinical services. Furthermore, college campuses offer several opportunities to implement screening and interventions. For example, large-scale screenings can be given for all incoming freshmen; students seen at health services, counseling centers, or local emergency rooms can receive a more specialized assessment and a determination for need for a brief intervention; various grievance systems for students who violate campus alcohol policies (e.g., housing) are opportunities to engage students. Naturally, there are several issues to address when implementing these clinical services, the most important being who should implement the screenings and interventions to students, and what training and supervision are needed. Nonetheless, established procedures have been validated and the potential is there for a college to readily implement them.

CHAPTER 5

IMPROVING THE QUALITY
OF POLICIES AND PROCEDURES

In the previous chapter, you learned about the value and role of appropriate intervention systems for college students whose drinking activities are impacting their physical and mental health. Such systems are critical for the well-being of these students, and they are an important part of addressing the health consequences of alcohol abuse.

However, even if you were able to intervene with and successfully treat every student who was addicted to alcohol, you would not change the culture that facilitates binge drinking and its consequences. Recall the following figure, which was presented in chapter 2. This figure points out the reality that interventions among the most serious problem users reach only a very few binge drinkers. The vast majority of the problems that result from alcohol use occur among students who are not the heaviest drinkers.

FIGURE 5.1

Triangle Framework of Responses for Individuals

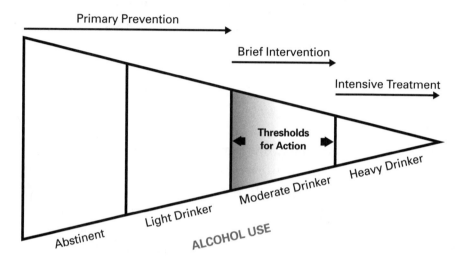

Most treatment is directed at the students near the point of the triangle. A useful metaphor, well known among prevention specialists,
bears repeating here.

> A doctor finds injured people washing up on the shore of a
> river. She keeps bringing them in, treating them, and letting
> them go. She gets better and better at triage and treatment,
> and soon sets up a very efficient system. She writes papers
> about it and gains fame for her wonderful system. Absorbed
> in doing great work, she never stops to walk upstream to find
> out what is causing all the injuries. Had she looked up, she
> would have seen that the addition of a rail on an upstream
> bridge would have prevented almost all the injuries.

This metaphor describes, to some degree, how schools deal with
alcohol problems on campus. School officials wait until they find the
worst cases—the alcoholic or the student injured in the course of binge

drinking—and then get those young people the kind of treatment they need. *Colleges don't pause to take a look at what's going on in the environment to cause the problem.*

This chapter helps the steering group and task force assess and improve the school's systems for dealing with the upstream problems. It addresses *strategy 2,* improve policies and procedures for addressing student alcohol issues. There are three parts to this strategy. First, you need to inventory the approaches you are currently using and understand the degree to which the research supports the effectiveness of those approaches. We recommend that you pursue interventions that have documented effectiveness. Second, you need to map out and align the systems you have—including the important connections among the various departments responsible for implementing the systems. And, finally, you need to be sure that you are properly and consistently enforcing the policies and practices across the campus—not looking the other way for certain student groups, and not letting some students fall through the cracks.

This chapter and the previous chapter work together to help you be sure that your campus has its systems in order. The systems in chapters 4 and 5 (strategies 1 and 2) are those over which you have the most direct influence.

Why Colleges Have Been Failing

Your first step will be to inventory existing programs. But before you begin, it's important to understand what is happening at campuses around the country—and what may be happening at your school. This section will help you understand why most schools are not seeing progress.

Your student population is vulnerable to binge drinking. Some students arrive on campus with a history of alcohol abuse. Most are coming into a brand-new environment, isolated from previous social ties, and with an urgent need to establish new ties. Yet the support they receive to help with this situation does not really fit well with their age and developmental state. Students are young adults, and they know that alcohol is one way to facilitate the development of new ties. It is readily available, it's cheap, and older peers can get it legally. It's no wonder that so many students use it. Acknowledging these effects and the instrumental use of alcohol is honest and doesn't neglect the fact that alcohol also causes significant problems for many students.

Efforts to reduce the vulnerability of young adults to alcohol have not succeeded. For example, increasing knowledge about the risks of alcohol, building skills for refusing alcohol, and promoting self-esteem do not appear to reduce the risk of alcohol abuse, at least on a wide scale. *College campuses* are conducive to using alcohol, simply because they include large numbers of young adults seeking to make new attachments. What have been demonstrated to be effective are actions that limit access to alcohol. Colleges need to restrict access to alcohol and allow students to find healthier ways to form these new attachments. Many of these opportunities to form new attachments already exist on most campuses, but they get overwhelmed by the lure of heavy drinking. Most schools have not addressed the alcohol sources that promote and sustain the heavy-drinking culture. Standard educational and programmatic approaches don't get at the core of the problem. This is why the culture doesn't change and why colleges don't make sustained reductions in drinking and its resulting harms.

Universities tend to stay focused on their own campus, while alcohol is primarily accessed off campus. Campus alcohol task forces repeat the things they are already good at: educating and providing services for students in need. These services are provided by people in housing, health services, student affairs, and so forth. Unfortunately, most of the services don't reduce student drinking, cover only a small portion of the student population, and often are not aligned well with other services. They have a narrow reach (dealing only with the most troubled individuals) and narrow effectiveness—hence low impact.

Colleges tend to put programs in place that serve a limited number of students and then focus on operating those programs well—even when the programs have limited success. Meanwhile, a program that is only modestly effective yet reaches the entire campus can do more than a program that is extremely effective but serves only one out of a thousand students. There's a simple, intuitive formula for this:

Impact = Effectiveness × Reach

The formula means that it may be better to do a broad number of modestly effective interventions that reach a lot of people than to implement a few excellent programs that serve only a few students. Even the most successful programs have their limits in terms of how effective they can be. A major error that many service providers make is that they concentrate on trying to improve effectiveness, doing something as well as it can be done, but only with a small group of students. The potential gains here in terms of impact are small. We recommend broadening the reach of effective interventions, even if it appears that the fidelity of delivery is not optimal. One example of this is expanding the use of brief motivational interviewing (BMI), which we discussed in chapter 4, to new settings, such as residence halls or the athletic department, by training the people who interact with students. It is likely that residence advisors or athletic trainers, two groups of people who could be trained to deliver BMI, will not be as effective in conducting these interventions as a trained counselor or psychologist. But the potential in terms of reach, and ultimately impact, can be much broader.

On a larger scale, policies can be effective because they apply to a much broader population—in theory, everyone. Even with modest effectiveness in terms of changing individual behavior, if they shift everyone's behavior a little bit, the potential impact on the population can be large.

Inventory Programs and Consider Impact

The first step, then, in implementing strategy 2 is to get a sense of what you are doing and consider the effectiveness of each program, process, or policy. It's still the case that a lot of the programs that campuses are trying fall within realms the college has full control over but that have undocumented and unlikely effectiveness.

The *inventory* of programs can be conducted fairly quickly. Ask all members of the task force to list the programs related to alcohol they are conducting, that they are aware of, or that they recall having been conducted in the past. Create a simple database, such as the one shown in table 5.1. Try to eliminate overlaps in the programs (that is, sometimes people call the same program by different names).

TABLE 5.1

Program Inventory

Set up a simple table such as the one below. List past or present alcohol programs on your campus, sponsoring department, dates of operation, and general attitude about impact. After completing the list, compare it to table 5.2, which shows the general impact of various types of programs typically offered on campuses.

PROGRAM	DEPARTMENT "HOME"	DATES OF OPERATION	IMPACT	WHAT THE RESEARCH SAYS	COMMENTS

Table 5.2 was created for this book. It shows typical campus programs and rates them on various factors: reach, effectiveness, cost, strength of evidence, and, finally, whether or not we recommend them.

TABLE 5.2

Impact of Typical Campus Practices

Below is a list of programs often offered on college campuses, with ratings of reach, effectiveness, cost, evidence for success, and our recommendations.

PROJECT, PROCESS, OR POLICY	REACH	COST	OUR RECOMMENDATION
Having a task force or coalition of groups concerned about alcohol use and consequences.			A task force can help promote change, but it is not sufficient. It can sometimes get in the way of progress.
Medical amnesty. This policy provides amnesty from sanctions when one student who is drinking against campus regulations helps another who is doing the same. (This is okay as a policy, but don't get bogged down discussing it; and recognize that it won't make much difference in the overall rates of drinking and related problems.)	low	low	This is a reasonable policy that reassures students that they will be treated fairly for doing the right thing and caretaking another student who needs help. It is important, however, that you don't send a message that students are not accountable for their behavior.
Recovery support, such as recovery residence halls, AA on campus, access to addictions professionals, peer programs to support students in recovery, and children of alcoholics programs.	low	high	This is a good thing to do, but it won't make a difference in the rates of drinking on campus.

continued on next page

TABLE 5.2

Impact of Typical Campus Practices

PROJECT, PROCESS, OR POLICY	REACH	COST	OUR RECOMMENDATION
Door-to-door community campaigns to connect students living off-site with their neighbors. (Community members like this, because their first experience isn't complaining about the student. And it is good for the students, as it establishes connection, reduces anonymity, and helps them see that they have an impact.) Impact depends on the number of students in off-campus housing.	low to moderate	moderate to high	This practice effectively communicates the standards you expect of students living in the community. It also provides a clear channel of communication between neighbors and the university and can alert the university to problems and help with community relations.
Off-campus housing risk management. In this process, campus housing professionals meet the landlords of off-campus housing and set up policies and rental agreements that pressure landlords to comply with occupancy and behavioral standards. (There is a lot of underage drinking at house parties—200 to 400 students may be served at one party.)	high	moderate to high	Creating policies for responsible behavior when living in off-campus rental units can help landlords keep students accountable.

continued on next page

TABLE 5.2

Impact of Typical Campus Practices

PROJECT, PROCESS, OR POLICY	REACH	COST	OUR RECOMMENDATION
Controls of alcohol service at university-sanctioned events. When a group is school-sanctioned, uses student fees, or is otherwise linked to the college, the college can set policies controlling alcohol use even when the group meets off campus. The school can put in place control policies such as using ID cards, registering events, requiring a supervising professional bartender, having security, and so forth for any event that uses university money or any group the university sponsors in some way.	modest	moderate	Having clear standards for alcohol service, including third-party vendors, can keep events where alcohol is sold under control.
Peer education. Many schools have peer-educator programs in which students are reached through their peers who are taught in a specific educational program. The effectiveness relates to the type of peer education. For example, brief motivational interviewing (noted below and described elsewhere in this book) is highly effective. But other types of education may be too broad, cover too many topics, and include a minimal amount of information about binge drinking. These programs are often done at booths, at special events, or at student housing (which may be the most effective setting for education-type programs).	low	high	Peer education programs are common at many schools, and the peer relationship can be used in concert with screening and brief intervention efforts, as well as education about policy and community standards on alcohol use and availability. Providing training in brief motivational interviewing and clear procedures for referring fellow students to needed services may be helpful.

continued on next page

TABLE 5.2

Impact of Typical Campus Practices

PROJECT, PROCESS, OR POLICY	REACH	COST	OUR RECOMMENDATION
Brief motivational interviewing. This technique is one of the recommended NIAAA methods. It's brief—like having your physician talk about good diet, smoking cessation, etc. Motivational interviewing may be part of peer education or used in other contexts. Because it is brief, you may reach a number of students with less effort.	moderate	high	Create a system to deliver brief motivational interviewing and work to increase its reach by having professional staff (e.g., housing supervisors, academic advisors, athletic trainers) deliver it.
Seminars and workshops as interventions. These are programs where the school brings in an expert, and students (or a subset of students such as athletes) are required to go. This is a popular intervention, but it can be costly (in time or speaker fees).	zero to low	high	Seminars or workshops by themselves are not very effective. Use these only as part of a strategic plan to get your staff trained to pursue effective interventions.
Alcohol summit. This involves multi-seminars. It can be useful as part of a kickoff for the alcohol task force to give everyone the same information. It is not very effective as an intervention method in student drinking. Effectiveness as a task force kickoff depends on the quality of the content; reach to students depends on the reach of the participating partners.	N/A	high	An alcohol summit is generally not very effective in promoting change. Use this approach to identify problems, start conversations with important stakeholders, and generate buy-in to pursuing effective interventions.

continued on next page

TABLE 5.2

Impact of Typical Campus Practices

PROJECT, PROCESS, OR POLICY	REACH	COST	OUR RECOMMENDATION
Follow-up for students in detox. This is a highly specific screen for students needing further intervention. Schools may get reports back on students who were transferred to detox. Some schools do nothing; others have a counselor put the student through alcohol diagnosis and employ disciplinary restrictions involving academic advisors, and they may also notify parents. Follow-up is good to do, but it will not reach many students.	low	high	We recommend tracking and follow-up with these students. Mapping these procedures on your campus can help with quality improvement at each step.
Training for resident assistants (RAs) in procedures to deal with alcohol-related problems. Incidences may involve vandalism, interpersonal conflict, and health consequences. This is useful but does not reduce binge drinking; it is a reactive intervention.	N/A	moderate to high	RAs can be trained in brief motivational interviewing skills and also appropriate procedures for referring at-risk students to appropriate services when necessary.
Care team for at-risk students. Involves health, housing, student affairs, Greek affairs, academic advising.	low	very high	A care team, especially one that cuts across different campus systems, can be helpful for ensuring that students get the help they need and don't fall through the cracks in the system. This is resource-intensive, requiring lots of time from highly skilled and paid professionals and likely won't impact the overall drinking environment at the school or in the community.

continued on next page

TABLE 5.2

Impact of Typical Campus Practices

PROJECT, PROCESS, OR POLICY	REACH	COST	OUR RECOMMENDATION
Schedule and market after-hours alternative events. These are widely used and may be favored by students on the task force, but they have very little effectiveness, as students attending are likely not to use alcohol anyway. They can also distract from more effective interventions because they don't compete with the perceived benefits of drinking. Marketing these as "alcohol-free alternatives" causes decreased attendance.	modest	moderate to high	We recommend that most of the responsibility for these events be given to interested and enthusiastic student groups. The coalition can support these activities but should not devote large amounts of resources to them. By themselves, these are typically ineffective for reducing drinking and associated problems.
Parental notification of student drinking. It can be effective to bring in a parent. Students really don't want their drinking issues reported to their parents. Parental opinion has been shown to be a strong influence on students, but informal surveys show that very few parents of problem drinkers have actually been notified.	very low	low	Parental notification has not been studied widely, but this policy may provide a channel for involving parents to a greater degree. Students are often highly motivated to avoid having to contact their parents about an alcohol violation so there may be some deterrence effect to this policy.
Twenty-first-birthday-card program. On some campuses, there are traditions involving a twenty-first-birthday bar crawl. This intervention features sending a birthday card reminding students to keep under control.	modest	modest	This program can be useful for raising awareness and can also serve as a channel for communications about policies, although this is unlikely to have a major effect by itself.

The programs, processes, and policies described in table 5.2 are common on college campuses. Compare them to those your campus is conducting (or has conducted in the past). You can see that some of the most popular programs are likely to have very little impact because of their combination of low reach and low effectiveness. Others may have very limited impact unless used strategically in concert with other initiatives.

In addition to comparing your programs, processes, and policies to the table, you can apply a public health analysis to them. In an excellent article on the principles of public health, Carol W. Runyan introduces a series of criteria that can be used to assess intervention strategies.[52] They include the following:

Effectiveness. Use interventions that at least have modest effectiveness; they don't have to be perfect. You need to consider effectiveness alongside reach.

Reach. Use interventions that hit a modest to large population—ideally, conditions that apply to everyone (pricing, availability). For example, athletic scholarship policies and amnesty policies have a low reach since they only apply to a few people in a certain situation. Some schools spend all of their efforts on interventions with limited reach. Be sure to incorporate interventions with broad reach on your campus.

Impact. This takes into account effectiveness and reach. Use interventions that have high potential for impact (Effectiveness × Reach).

Cost. Cost includes both financial and time investment (the cost of trained implementers). For example, a financially low-cost intervention may still be considered costly if it requires lots of staff time. Resource availability—for example, the presence (or absence) of a community organizer on staff—can play a major role in influencing your selection of strategies.

Freedom. Many public health interventions curtail rights. You need to explore the degree to which this will occur for any intervention you consider. When an intervention impinges freedom, think about how you will advocate for the reduction in freedom given the benefits to public health.

Equity. Are all people treated the same across the intervention? For example, athletes can sometimes receive exceptional treatment. Real or not, perceptions of fairness influence the effectiveness of an intervention.

Stigmatization. Will the intervention create stigma for a certain group or make the group readily identifiable?

Community and individual preferences. People may prefer to implement certain strategies, even ineffective ones, because they are comfortable with that approach or have experience with it in other settings. Acknowledging "what you want" is a criterion that can be helpful; it is more intellectually honest to get your preference out in the open.

Feasibility. An intervention may be known to be highly effective, but not feasible given current conditions. For example, the absence of public support can make a sensible intervention less feasible. It is important to choose your battles carefully and save your political capital for interventions that are the most effective.

You can analyze your own systems using the criteria above. To do so, you need to collect measures and the indicators of success, for both the process and outcomes. Use that data, in combination with the recommendations in table 5.2, to analyze your current activities.

This is a major effort. No intervention will be rated highly on all these categories. Many popular strategies affect only a few students and have not been shown to be effective. This is not to say you shouldn't pursue some of these strategies. They may be very important to a segment of your students, and research may eventually demonstrate that these strategies are effective. However, if your campus is *only* pursuing these types of strategies, you should add ones that have broad reach and are effective.

We encourage you to focus on strategies that have potential for high impact. An honest assessment can also help you articulate why you have not previously pursued some of the environmental interventions recommended by us and others. Perhaps by systematically applying Dr. Runyan's criteria, you will find that some of the most effective policies have other benefits or that their alleged drawbacks (the reasons you have not considered or vigorously pursued them in the past) are not as serious as they first appeared.

Finally, most of the programs in table 5.2 do not add up to a comprehensive system, because few of those listed work to change the environment. Some schools have components of a comprehensive system, but they don't have good alignment among the components. It's the whole and the comprehensiveness that ultimately matter. The steering group will need to align the systems it has while it adds new systems that offer greater impact. The lack of alignment is another reason why schools haven't seen much success. In the next section, we'll look at how the systems can be aligned.

Aligning and Improving Systems

You now know what the programs, policies, and processes on your campus look like. Next you need to align these systems to produce the maximum benefit. There are three steps in this process. First, you need to map the flow of the major interventions you offer. Then you need to map the connections among the various interventions. And, finally, you need to use that information to determine where gaps exist and how to fill them—to ensure large numbers of students are not falling between the cracks.

Mapping Programs, Processes, and Policies

Mapping programs includes answering the following questions:

- What current programs do we have in place to address alcohol use and its associated problems?
- What kinds of individual interventions do we use?
- What kinds of environmental interventions do we use?
- What processes do we utilize with students who are experiencing problems with alcohol or drawing attention to themselves as a result of their alcohol use?
- How consistent are we in implementing those programs and processes across student groups? (For example, do we treat elite athletes differently than other students?)
- What is our campus history and what are our campus norms regarding alcohol use? How have these been shaped over time? Do we have written records or oral histories of previous attempts to change drinking behavior? Can we change these conditions moving forward?

As you answer these questions, you can begin to develop process maps (or procedure analyses) of your most important activities. A procedure analysis for key processes can help you understand where the process is helping, where it is not, and where you can evaluate changes in the future. Such an analysis lays out a road map for quality improvement.

Creating a Process Map

Figure 5.2 shows a process map developed at the University of Minnesota.

FIGURE 5.2

Process Map for Managing an Intoxicated Student[53]

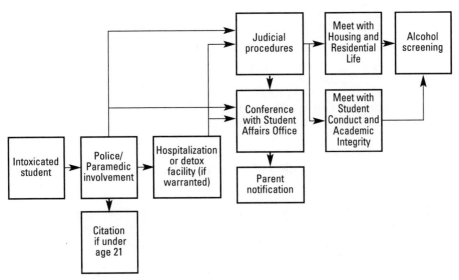

The figure shows the various steps that occur when a student is reported as intoxicated at the University of Minnesota. Such a process map is incredibly useful in several ways. First, it reveals the various branch points where decisions are made. Each of these points can be opportunities for improving a process.

Second, the map helps show other departments and staff how one program works. This becomes useful in mapping the connections among programs. These connections are very important, as missed connections result in students falling through the cracks. They may also reveal where policies and procedures are inconsistent with one another.

Third, such maps, by showing the areas where individual judgment on the part of staff occurs, may reveal gaps in enforcement or the consistency of enforcement.

Finally, the maps can be helpful for evaluation and quality improvement. You can use these maps to quantify the number of students who reach a specific decision point, set goals for improvement, make policy or procedural changes based on those goals, track subsequent performance, and measure whether those modifications improve the outcomes you want to change.

Creating such maps for your college need not be tedious. Start with the one here and revise it to fit your current programs. Different maps can be created for specific programs. For example, figure 5.3 shows a series of steps involved in screening students for high-risk drinking at the University of Minnesota.

FIGURE 5.3

Screening of High-Risk Drinkers[54]

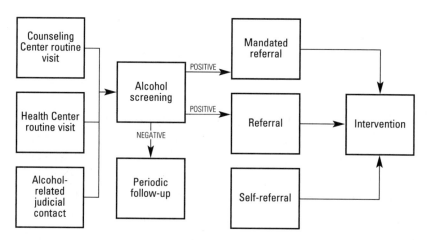

In addition to mapping the programs and processes in use on campus, the task force should map programs and processes that occur in the community surrounding the campus. This might include police systems, local health care resources, and so forth. In essence, every constituent group represented on the task force can create a map of its most important processes for intervening with students. Typical groups off campus might include

- neighborhood association (for example, process for reporting alcohol use at off-campus student housing)

- local politicians (to support improving or strengthening regulations and policies)
- police (for example, disposition of underage students found drinking at bars; enforcement of server regulations)
- local hospital (detox processes, including relationship between hospital and student health service)
- chamber of commerce (for example, process for street cleanup after bar hours)

Mapping Connections

It is not enough to simply map the programs, processes, and policies regarding alcohol consumption. You also need to map the connections among these elements and among the people who implement them. Missing connections are opportunities for students to get lost in the system. They may be evidence of the covert means by which the culture perpetuates binge drinking. The gaps are opportunities for identifying inequitable treatment of individuals or groups of individuals. The connections may also reveal differences from one system to the next in how a problem is dealt with. Such differences in processes can create extra difficulties when trying to navigate systems. Here are questions to explore.

- How are our systems connected? (Refer to your list of programs, developed in table 5.1, as you assess connections.)
- What is the integration across different systems? For example, how well does housing interface with health care? How well does the student affairs office interface with the community police department?
- How often and by what process do the individuals in differing programs communicate with each other about the students they service?

Don't Be Overwhelmed

Mapping programs and connections among them may sound daunting. Don't fret.

First, remember that the task force will be working at this for some years; you don't have to do everything at once.

Second, the work should be parsed out among the constituent members. For example, the neighborhood association can identify and map any of its relevant processes, as can the campus health service. Rely on the wisdom of constituents to determine which processes need to be mapped.

Third, use the expertise you have on campus. Process mapping is a common technique used in business. Faculty may have specialized software to help with this task. Students can also be very helpful in using technology to facilitate development of these maps. Several software tools are available specifically for this purpose, although they can also be created using standard software for both PC and Mac applications.

Finally, the work of uncovering connections can be done during presentations to the entire stakeholder group. For example, if you've identified fifteen programs or processes, you can set aside time at each meeting for the process "owner" to describe its process, and then have the group itself discuss the connections among processes.

The work of understanding these connections is very important and is one of the outcomes of the task force. As you uncover connections, you'll figure out how to close gaps in the system, so you can serve more troubled students and reduce the negative consequences of binge drinking.

Developing Effective Systems for Alcohol Control Policies

In our research, we have found some striking inconsistencies across the systems that exist within schools. The biggest of these inconsistencies are schools that have policies on the books, but uneven or no enforcement. This creates a major problem for them. First, unenforced or inconsistently enforced policies put the school at greater risk in lawsuits. Second, lax enforcement sends a strong message to the culture that the problem the policy is supposed to address is not really a problem.

There are several common components of implementing effective policies. It is helpful to consider all of them together in a process of reframing. This process may help you identify breakdowns in your current systems and areas for improvement. By using similar language, reframing can also help you align your efforts to reduce student alcohol use with your larger university mission.

Reframing Your Thinking about Policy

Colleges and college communities have been reluctant to engage in alcohol control policy work, despite clear evidence that those strategies are very effective for reducing binge drinking and the consequences that result. We think that one reason for this is the way policy is viewed by college professionals. People in student development are often on the front lines of addressing student alcohol issues. These are professionals whose training and mission is to promote positive development for students. In our experience, these people love working on a college campus with students and are committed to providing a positive place for them to grow and have new experiences. They don't want to be viewed by those same students as the "fun police," bent on restricting students' experience. Policies can easily be viewed as punishing students. More policies and more enforcement simply translate into more punishment that administrators have to be responsible for carrying out. It is natural and understandable that those who are charged with addressing student drinking don't want to take on this role.

Reframing policies is an important step toward enacting those that are effective, and finding common ground is important. Policy is really about formally codifying standards within the university about the consumption and provision of alcohol. If you think about policy in this way, you can turn it toward a more positive perspective. A university community should aspire to ambitious goals for educating its students and serving the community at large. Heavy alcohol use and an environment where heavy use occurs regularly are often directly inconsistent with these aspirations.

Establish a clear statement about the university's standards and the kind of common community that facilitates those goals. Many universities already have these statements. Then frame your policies in a way that helps create the conditions that you want to promote. Keep in mind that community standards can be about both individual behavior and the behavior of organizations.

Now that you are looking at policy in a new way, let's consider the features of a good policy. Policy is made up of several components. Policy is usually thought of as the written policy itself. This is the formalization of community standards, but it is only a small part of the different features of a policy.

The *design* of a policy is critical. A good policy is written in ways that effectively communicate the community standard it codifies and facilitate the ability of individuals to comply with its intent. Many policies contain loopholes, so that some individuals or organizations are not fully accountable. Some of this is intentional and some of it is unintentional, but good policy design seeks to avoid such loopholes and gaps.

People who are affected by a policy need *education* about what the policy is, whom it applies to and when, how to comply with the policy, and the consequences imposed for not complying. This is not education in the typical sense of talking about the risks of alcohol. Education can also be conducted to let people in the community know about the policy and all of its provisions, how they will be held accountable to those standards, and how they can comply with the policy.

For example, highway patrol departments in many states engage in major public communication efforts to let people know when they are cracking down on drinking and driving. These efforts show effective policy and enforcement education at work. The idea is not to try to catch as many people as possible, but to send a message about the likelihood of being caught. These efforts have been very effective in reducing alcohol-impaired driving, which ultimately is the goal. Good policy implementation is supported with effective communication.

Some policies require the development of new *skills* to comply with the policy. For example, those who serve alcohol in licensed establishments need to know how to effectively refuse sales. The way a server speaks to a customer and seeks support from the bar's manager in dealing with an intoxicated patron requires specific abilities that can be learned, practiced, and improved. Identify and provide the skills that are needed to effectively comply with the policy. Universities can play an important role in developing trainings to educate about policy and evaluating their effectiveness.

Enforcement is really about creating accountability to the community standards. As mentioned previously, many campus officials want to avoid enforcement, viewing it as synonymous with punishing students. Enforcement should not only focus on individual consumers of alcohol. It may be more effective to address enforcement efforts toward those who supply alcohol and make sure they comply with established community standards.

Many policy initiatives focus primarily on increasing the severity of the punishment, with the idea that the greater the severity of punishment, the less likely the behavior is to occur. However, deterrence is more complicated than this.

There are three important components of policy enforcement. One is *severity of punishment*, which is perhaps the least important of the three. High severity of punishment can oftentimes undermine enforcement because those responsible for the enforcement may avoid implementation. The other components of policy enforcement are *certainty* of the punishment and the *celerity* (or swiftness) of the punishment. Increasing the likelihood of punishment will help ensure that more of those who are not in compliance with community standards are accountable. The more quickly the punishment follows the violation, the more effective the enforcement effort is for decreasing the occurrence of violations in the community. You can examine your policies and procedures and work to make it more likely that violators will be caught and that the punishment will be delivered quickly. If the severity of the punishment may deter you from implementing the consequences in a consistent and fair way, you may even consider reducing the severity of the punishment.

Overcoming Objections to Implementing Environmental Interventions

Seeking to change the conditions that promote heavy drinking on your campus or in your community is difficult. One important obstacle you will have to overcome will be the objections raised to the types of approaches we recommend. We have found that you can anticipate many of these objections. That will allow you to be prepared to counter them. Below are some of the most common objections, and some comments on how to counter them.

If only all underage students could drink, we would not have such a big problem.

The minimum legal drinking age of twenty-one in the United States is one of the most effective and well-studied alcohol control policies in existence. This policy has led to dramatic declines in drinking, as well as in alcohol-related traffic fatalities, among teenagers over the past forty years. The raising of the minimum legal drinking age is one of the most important public health advances of the late twentieth century.

While some college presidents have advocated for a return to nineteen or eighteen as the minimum age, this would be a public health disaster. It would simply shift the problem into high schools and lead to an increase in drinking and all the negative consequences that come with it among college students.

Dropping the legal drinking age would not make addressing college-student drinking easier; it would make it harder. Keep in mind, the drinking age not only prohibits underage youth from drinking or purchasing alcohol, it prevents those who sell alcohol from selling and marketing to youth. A change in policy will mean more availability of alcohol to younger people and more aggressive marketing. The truth is, researchers already know the results of this experiment—lowering the drinking age means more drinking among those who are younger, and more of the problems associated with drinking in the community. Decreasing the minimum drinking age will not make college students drink more responsibly. There is no need to repeal the law and needlessly risk lives. Spend your time pursuing other policies and encouraging your task force members to do the same.[55]

We can't be viewed as the fun police. Students won't seek us out for help if they think our purpose is to monitor and punish them.
This is an understandable sentiment. Most college administrators didn't choose their career path to become rule enforcers. But any community needs to set standards for what is and what is not acceptable behavior. Much of the problematic drinking behavior among college students is not (or at least should not be) acceptable behavior. Like every community, college communities need standards for behavior, and accountability for adhering to those standards. We recommend using this language to talk about alcohol control policies in your community. Ultimately, no one wants the negative consequences of alcohol that you seek to reduce and avoid. Keep the conversation focused on the negative consequences of alcohol, including the secondhand effects of drinking that happen to

non-drinkers. Framed this way, policies that are effective can be more acceptable to your community.

I don't want to punish good students.

By and large, *all* students are good kids. Work to set standards for behavior that create a better environment for all. Students need to be accountable for behavior that puts themselves and others at risk. Keep in mind that punishments need not be severe to be effective. Work on improving the likelihood that students who don't adhere to community standards will be noticed, and work to make whatever consequences are appropriate in your community occur quickly after the violation. These factors will help deter other students from making similar violations. Sometimes lightening up on the severity of the punishment can be helpful in this context (see our discussion earlier in this chapter). Working with students in advance to decide on appropriate severity of punishment and involving students in judicial procedures can also be very helpful.

Accountability to standards is important, but keep in mind that these don't all have to be directed at individual students. Effective environmental interventions address the supply and suppliers of alcohol. Accountability for community standards for alcohol service is very important and should be a focus of your efforts to reduce student alcohol use.

We'll just be pushing the drinking somewhere else.

Displacement is a major concern of college task force members who are considering various policy initiatives. Displacement is the notion that cracking down on heavy drinking in a specific area, for example in the residence halls, will simply move the same level of drinking to other locations, including locations that create conditions that place students at even higher risk. This concern is a theoretical concern, and one that has been examined in several studies but has not been demonstrated. But whether displacement does occur in practice, the key is the net effect—whether the situation improves overall or if it is worse. When this issue has been examined in research studies, there is clear evidence that the overall effect is less drinking and fewer problems.[56]

If you suspect that your interventions may result in displacement, monitor and assess whether or not that is the case. If you can hypothesize the displacement effect, be intentional about collecting data to determine this. If you see evidence of displacement, this is an opportunity to develop an intervention to help mitigate that displacement.

The alcohol industry is too strong. We are not prepared to take on the political establishment.

Many college administrators feel very uncomfortable about engaging in political action, especially on policies that may be controversial in their community. Find out whether you have people with strong political or organizing skills on your task force. If not, get appropriate training for your members or go out and recruit some to join you and lead the charge. Finding people with these skills may be easier than you think.

There is strong public sentiment against interventions to reduce alcohol availability.

Don't automatically assume that this is the case. Particularly in communities where heavy alcohol use is a major problem, you may find greater public support for effective alcohol control interventions than you expect. Don't guess—collect the data. See the resources we provide on assessing public opinion in your community (documents 3 and 4 on the CD-ROM) and find experts at your college or in your community who can help you get high-quality public opinion data. This information is very powerful for encouraging decision makers to enact effective policies and procedures.

We can control alcohol on campus. But we can't influence the availability of alcohol in the community. It's not our job.

Often those who have been charged to work on alcohol issues on campus have experience and training in education and student development. The skills for implementing policy change and policy enforcement are not the skills of people working on this issue on campus. That is different from not being able to influence change in the community. Training can help get those who are working on the issues on campus up to speed if they are committed to taking an environmental approach. If campus staff are not interested in making that commitment, you can find and hire people who are. These new people with new skills should not threaten work on individual-focused interventions. Move past any conflict between individually focused and environmental approaches and embrace a broader approach. Reject the notion that environmental interventions are in conflict with individual interventions. You need both. Working on individual interventions can help facilitate environmental interventions.

Systems Alignment

Making a commitment to align your systems and implement environmental interventions may require a fundamental shift in your thinking about the issue. This shift is challenging, in part because the approach to environmental change is a very different way of thinking about the problem. It is very important (and the main theme of this book) to employ *both* ways of thinking, from an individual perspective and from an environmental perspective as well.

The language of individual approaches often differs considerably from that of environmental approaches. Empirically based individual approaches emphasize methods that encourage individuals to reconsider the ways they think. The process is one that encourages insight into oneself. It is not proscriptive in the sense that the intervention tells students what they should and should not do. Rather, the emphasis is on realigning their thinking and behavior to match their goals and the best aspirations for themselves. Responsibility for change remains with the individual.

Environmental interventions are often more proscriptive, with right and wrong ways to do things. In this book, we describe alcohol policy as a *codification of community standards* for the use and sale of alcohol. Viewed in this sense, communities have an opportunity to engage in this same alignment process about the standards for alcohol consumption and service. Having good data available—like the data we recommend that you collect—can help you ask the question to members of your community, Is this acceptable in our community?

If it is not, you have the tools to adopt new standards and methods for getting community members to comply with those standards.

CASE EXAMPLE

A RIOT BECOMES AN OPPORTUNITY

A riot involving three hundred University of Vermont students became an opportunity for change on campus. The riot occurred as bars were emptying, and resulted in property damage, arrests, negative press coverage, and, eventually, a discussion of the role of student drinking in the riot.

The campus alcohol coalition was able to capitalize on the incident to push for changes. The incident put student drinking front and center in the community. University leadership began discussions with the mayor's office. Several summit meetings were held, which resulted in action plans. Although the coalition and the mayor's office did not have the personnel or resources to follow through on the plan, and the number of follow-through tasks were unrealistic, the incident still sparked improvements in how the campus and community dealt with the problem of binge drinking, including

- an increase in the number of community members participating in discussions of the issue
- increased student involvement

continued on next page

- action over blame—the discussions moved from finger-pointing to figuring out how to solve the problem
- an increased understanding that high-risk drinking is an environmental problem rather than just one of misbehavior
- increased capacity to respond
- city involvement in the alcohol coalition. The mayor joined the steering committee and cooperation increased between the city and the university.

These developments set the stage for subsequent action and progress. There are several lessons here. First, be prepared to capitalize on the opportunities inherent in these kinds of events. Second, when making action plans, keep the plans in line with the resources and the passion of the participants—and be sure to have a coordinator to see them through. And, finally, remember that even when immediate plans fail, forward motion can still result.[57]

Chapter Summary

In this chapter, you learned about the very serious work of getting your campus house in order. We hope that you have mapped the various systems, services, and policies in place and discussed the connections among these overt elements of the campus culture—the stated rules and the systems that perpetuate the culture's stance toward alcohol.

This step is essential as the task force prepares to move forward. You don't have to complete it, but you do need to be well on your way with it as you move to the next strategies. The coming strategies push the task force deeper into the community. This is part of the reason why you want to have successes getting your internal policies, practices, and enforcements aligned. Such alignment is difficult, yet it largely involves elements that are completely (or almost completely) under the control of the campus. As you reach further into the community, you will be working to influence rather than set policy, and working to support (or demand) enforcement rather than carry it out yourself.

CHAPTER 6

RESTRICTING ALCOHOL ACCESS

The two most effective strategies a college can pursue to change heavy alcohol consumption behaviors among its students are to restrict access to alcohol and to increase its price.

Both of these strategies are difficult. A task force can make some small changes to how alcohol is served or made available to students on campus, but by and large success relies on the task force's willingness to reach beyond the campus borders—often far beyond the campus borders—to influence policy at the local and state levels.

In this chapter, we focus on *strategy 3*, limit the availability of alcohol by reducing marketing and outlet density and by improving responsible service standards; and *strategy 4*, enforce existing policies on underage drinking, service to intoxicated patrons, and alcohol-impaired driving. The strategies combine to *restrict alcohol access on and near campus*. The tactics required to implement these strategies are closer to home and, therefore, many alcohol task forces find them easier to execute. Chapter 7 will focus on strategy 5, increase alcohol pricing.

Strategies 3 and 4 are two sides of one coin. They call for (1) *creating policies* that reduce the physical and social availability of alcohol; and (2) *enforcing regulations* that act as physical and social barriers. Both are critical. In fact, many communities already have useful policies in place, but may simply ignore them or enforce them inconsistently. The combination of these two approaches helps reduce student access to alcohol. We have separated them in the treatment here, but you will note that discussions of policy often include information on enforcement and vice versa. Before exploring these two approaches, we will explore the concepts of physical and social availability.

Reducing the Availability of Alcohol

Physical availability refers to the alcohol outlets near campus; the places where alcohol can be obtained. *Social availability* is a more complicated concept; it refers to the ways in which students can obtain alcohol through their social contacts. It also includes community standards for tolerance or intolerance toward illegal consumption, public intoxication, and the disruptions associated with these issues. Social availability can be influenced by written regulations and their enforcement and in the unwritten norms about what is accessible; the ease of access at bars, liquor stores, house parties, and frat parties; and the readiness of legal-age individuals to procure alcohol for friends and for underage students.

The following tactics influence physical and social availability through regulatory efforts. We have listed them (roughly) in order of the degree to which colleges have influence over them. Some tactics can be implemented with specific campus organizations, such as campus housing and fraternity houses. Other tactics involve decisions about policies, priorities, and resources that other institutions and agencies must make, but that can be influenced by colleges. While some of the first tactics listed are more directly controlled by college officials, those farther down the list tend to influence the behavior of more people and be more effective on a population level. The task force should seek to address as many of these policy tactics as it can handle; they work together. Prioritize them (along with your enforcement efforts) both by looking at what you can do quickly and easily and by looking at the eventual impact. Remember that you're in this for the long haul, and so can keep pushing along in some areas. Keep in mind, too, that the forces that profit from and promote alcohol consumption also have reason to continue their efforts—you can't let up. Patience and persistence are your allies.

- Control alcohol at college-affiliated housing and events by banning alcohol or adopting best practices for serving.
- Implement server training.
- Implement social host party laws.
- Restrict public alcohol consumption.
- Restrict hours of sale.
- Restrict days of sale.
- Reduce advertising.
- Implement and enforce keg registration.
- Reduce the number and density of outlets and licenses.
- Use a "local option" on controls (or lobby for one if you don't have it).

Controlling Alcohol at College-affiliated Housing and Events

Heavy alcohol consumption and the problems that result in college settings can occur at Greek parties, in college-owned-and-affiliated housing, in privately owned housing that caters to students, and in nearby neighborhoods in which students rent. Colleges have varying degrees of leverage in these settings. When the housing is owned by the college or the organization is sanctioned by the college, it can take several actions.

- Limit the amount of alcohol served.
- Require parties to register.
- Require guest lists and enforce them.
- Require fraternities to bear the liability instead of the college (when the fraternity houses are owned by the college).
- Require a security person and sobriety monitors.
- Restrict other entry points so that all guests can be monitored.
- Partner with the national chapter of the association to which the housing organization is attached to institute a

variety of risk management practices including prevention of underage service and over-service and education on the risk of acquaintance rape and assault.

Most locales have ordinances that hold social hosts responsible if their guests become intoxicated and cause damage, parallel to the retail dram shop laws, but often with sterner consequences. The local police find these very helpful when enforcing controls on house parties. (See also the discussion of social host laws on page 135.)

Risk Management at Greek Organizations

The Interfraternity Council at the University of Minnesota adopted a restrictive set of policies to manage risk and reduce alcohol problems among members and at events held at fraternity-owned buildings. This policy document was informed by similar policies at other universities and can be adapted for use at your university. The entire risk management policy can be seen in document 7 on the CD-ROM. It includes policies requiring

- ▶ event registration, facilitated by an online form
- ▶ use and filing of preprinted guest lists, including guest-to-member ratio limitations
- ▶ limitations on events in which alcohol will be available
- ▶ use of sober monitors and door monitors
- ▶ proof of age and identification
- ▶ alcohol "check-in" systems for managing "bring your own beverage" practices; for

continued on next page

example, all fraternity events at the University of
Minnesota have become bring your own alcohol
(BYOB) events due to liability involved in illegal
provision of alcohol

There are many other requirements. We've excerpted the
alcohol policy on pages 132–33. Please see the entire policy,
as many other sections also have an impact on alcohol access
and consumption. The combined effect of these policies has
been to reduce the number of attendees at parties, particularly
those individuals who were not invited and may not be known
to members of the house. Undergraduates at the University
of Minnesota who are not members now know that they
won't be able to access alcohol at a fraternity party.

There are more restrictive policies that could have additional impacts, but these are policies developed by members
of the Greek organizations as their own community
standards. The policies effectively get fraternity houses to
stop functioning as de facto bars for large groups of students
under the legal drinking age. Monitoring of these policies by
the task force may help keep Greek organizations accountable
to their own standards, or help them set standards that are
more in line with the rest of the university community. These
policies may not reduce heavy drinking among members of
Greek organizations or those who attend their parties, but
they will likely reduce the service of alcohol to other students
(many of whom are under the legal drinking age) who otherwise might have attended the parties, and reduce the likelihood that the parties become out of control.

ALCOHOL POLICY[58]

A. The possession, sale, use, or consumption of ALCOHOLIC BEVERAGES, while on chapter premises or during a fraternity event, in any situation sponsored or endorsed by the chapter, or at any event an observer would associate with the fraternity, must be in compliance with any and all applicable laws of the state, province, county, city and institution of higher education, and must comply with either the BYOB or Third Party Vendor Guidelines.

B. No alcoholic beverages may be purchased through or with chapter funds nor may the purchase of same for members or guests be undertaken or coordinated by any member in the name of or on behalf of the chapter. The purchase or use of a bulk quantity or common source(s) of alcoholic beverage, for example, kegs or cases, is prohibited.

C. OPEN PARTIES, meaning those with unrestricted access by non-members of the fraternity, without specific invitation, where alcohol is present, are prohibited.

D. No members, collectively or individually, shall purchase for, serve to, or sell alcoholic beverages to any minor (i.e., those under legal drinking age).

E. The possession, sale or use of any ILLEGAL DRUGS or CONTROLLED SUBSTANCES while on chapter premises or during a fraternity event or at any event that an observer would associate with the fraternity is strictly prohibited.

F. No chapter may co-sponsor an event with an alcohol distributor or tavern (tavern defined as an establishment generating more than half of annual gross sales from alcohol) at which alcohol is given away, sold or otherwise provided to those present. This includes any event held in, at or on the

continued on next page

property of a tavern as defined above for purposes of fundraising. However, a chapter may rent or use a room or area in a tavern as defined above for a closed event held within the provisions of this policy, including the use of a third party vendor and guest list. An event at which alcohol is present may be conducted or co-sponsored with a charitable organization if the event is held within the provisions of this policy.

G. No chapter may co-sponsor, co-finance or attend or participate in a function at which alcohol is purchased by any of the host chapters, groups or organizations.

H. All recruitment or rush activities associated with any chapter will be non-alcoholic. No recruitment or rush activities associated with any chapter may be held at or in conjunction with a tavern or alcohol distributor as defined in this policy.

I. No member or pledge, associate/new member or novice shall permit, tolerate, encourage or participate in "drinking games." The definition of drinking games includes but is not limited to the consumption of shots of alcohol, liquor or alcoholic beverages, the practice of consuming shots equating to one's age, "beer pong," "century club," "dares" or any other activity involving the consumption of alcohol which involves duress or encouragement related to the consumption of alcohol.

J. No alcohol shall be present at any pledge/associate member/new member/novice program, activity or ritual of the chapter. This includes but is not limited to activities associated with "bid night," "big brother/big sister night" and initiation.

K. No drinking apparatuses may be present at any restricted event.

Implementing Server Training

Many states and localities have dram shop laws, which hold establishments and individual servers legally responsible for damage caused by customers to whom they served alcohol. Good server training and management risk training can reduce the prevalence of service to underage people and to intoxicated patrons. Alcohol establishments are usually motivated to provide this training, because the training helps promote good service practices that protect them from dram shop liability. Such training may help keep insurance costs down for these establishments as well.

But training for servers and managers is complex. Most outlets have rapid turnover in server staff. If they conduct training once or twice a year, there's a good chance that new staff will never be trained—the ones most likely to fail to check age or recognize signs of intoxication.

Typically, bars hire consultants who have a private business to do this training. But since such in-person trainings are not frequent, many staff miss them. This is an area where colleges can apply their native skills in education. For example, the University of Nebraska–Lincoln developed an online server training program for those who sell and serve alcohol in Nebraska.[59] A newly hired staff person can log in to the system, go through an online training program, learn about personal liabilities according to state laws, and learn correct alcohol service practices.

In many locales, server training is voluntary; in some, it is mandatory, a condition of the alcohol license. When server training is mandatory, underage service and service to intoxicated people tend to decline. As few as ten years ago, an underage drinker was served three out of four times. Server training, legal restrictions, and enforcement have combined to reduce the prevalence to roughly one out of four times. Unfortunately, there has not been as much improvement in reductions of service to intoxicated patrons. Both areas represent business opportunities for institutions with educational expertise.

Creating (or Enforcing) Social Host Laws

Social host regulations are parallel to the dram shop laws that hold alcohol establishment owners responsible for harm caused by intoxicated customers. In the case of social hosting laws, when intoxicated or underage service occurs at a private party and the guest leaves and causes harm, the host can be held liable for the damage. Knowledge of such laws and the penalties, which may be much more severe than their counterparts on the commercial side, has a great deterrent effect. These policies are gaining momentum. Neighborhood associations often support such laws, especially in neighborhoods with high rates of student rentals. The neighborhood group can take the lead in encouraging the city to adopt such laws, and contacting the police to enforce them.

State laws on social hosting liabilities vary widely. Some states do not impose any liability on social hosts. Those states with limits vary the liability ranging from injuries that occur only on the host's premises to injuries that occur anywhere a guest who has consumed alcohol goes. And many states have laws that pertain specifically to furnishing alcohol to minors. To find the laws in your state, see the Alcohol Policy Information System (APIS) at www.alcoholpolicy.niaaa.nih.gov. Note, though, that social host laws are mostly local and many will not be reflected in the APIS database. Be sure to check the laws for your community as well.

Kansas has passed and amended a social host state law during the past decade. "Paul's Law" is named for a teenager who was killed while driving home from a friend's party where he and other teenagers had been drinking. The friend's parents were home during the party while the teens drank alcohol. Paul's mother worked to get the social host law passed. It established a new crime of "unlawfully hosting" parties at which persons younger than eighteen were served, and established a minimum fine of $1,000. Subsequent amendments raised the age to twenty-one and improved other aspects of the law.[60]

The publication *Model Social Host Liability Ordinance*, available from Ventura County in California, provides a model ordinance with legal commentary that you can adapt for your local community.[61]

Restricting Public Alcohol Consumption

Most communities have restrictions on public alcohol consumption. When enforced, these are a good, reasonably effective means of restricting access. Campuses can ban open containers in public areas, place restrictions on hallways in residence halls, and so forth. The public laws become quite useful when patrons start to spill out of local bars near campus or other places where drinkers are congregating. This atmosphere can be a public hazard and nuisance, and also sends a message of social tolerance for public intoxication. When an ordinance is in place, it is also an opportunity for police enforcement. In some campus communities, the streets become a public drinking zone after big sporting events. In these situations, colleges can push for an open container law if one is not already in place. (Open container laws are also relevant for automobiles and useful for drinking that occurs in association with campus sporting events; all but six states have such restrictions.)

Restricting Hours of Sale

Late bar hours contribute to intoxication; people stay out later, have more to drink, are more intoxicated when they leave, and are more likely to cause problems as a result. Studies in communities that increased their hours of sale by two or more hours show an increase in drinking, fighting, injuries, drinking and driving, motor vehicle crashes, and emergency room admissions.[62] In locales that are considering extensions of bar hours, colleges should advocate against such changes. However, it is probably not a high priority to take on the fight of restricting currently established practices; other tactics can be more fruitful than trying to undo established norms.

Restricting Days of Sale

Limiting the days of sale, usually banning sales on Sunday, is an effective policy, and retail outlets may support it. The small shops like the day off and the uniform law creates an even playing field among competitors.

Some states are considering dropping these restrictions. If this is the case in your state, it is good use of the task force's time to lobby against dropping them. The alcohol task force must always keep watch on the opposition's efforts to relax regulation even as the task force seeks to advocate for and implement new policies.

Reducing Advertising

The campus can ban ads for alcohol in the campus newspaper, ban flier distributions on campus, and push to restrict billboard and other forms of public advertising near campus. There is no scientific evidence of large impact from this intervention, but reductions in alcohol advertising can reduce the social acceptability of alcohol and make room for other options.

There are voluntary industry standards regarding alcohol advertising. The publication *Code of Responsible Practices for Beverage Alcohol Advertising and Marketing,* available from the Distilled Spirits Council of the United States, contains guidelines that cover placement of ads and their content.[63] These include a guideline recommending that promotions for alcohol products should not be placed in college or university newspapers or on college campuses. Another guideline relates to degrading or sexually oriented messages or images. It can be helpful to know the industry standards and monitor local retailers for compliance. The publication contains information about how to file a complaint.

Local restrictions on advertising are frequently unenforced, but the alcohol task force can work for this. Some states or localities restrict the distance an alcohol advertisement can be from a school or church. You can map the location of billboards and other public ads, observe the ad content, and then check the regulations and push for enforcement. Though the impact on overall drinking will not be large, the success at enforcing these regulations can prepare the campus coalition for more ambitious and effective efforts. This can be a fun project for students who are looking to make a visible impact in the community.

Requiring Keg Registration

The college has excellent leverage over college housing and college-approved organizations; it can disallow kegs or develop rules that tightly restrict use. The college also has reasonable leverage over off-campus rental housing. It can encourage those who have the authority to set keg registration policies, often working with the local neighborhood associations and police, who are usually quite aware of the trouble spots.

Keg registration is required by some communities, and it can be a useful tactic. First, it can serve as a deterrent; those who buy a keg realize that they may be monitored. And second, when infractions occur, registration can provide supporting evidence for enforcement. If underage drinkers are found at (or having just left) a party with a keg, the police have good evidence to hold the host liable, and the courts may apply severe penalties. Both of these can help reduce social provision at house and fraternity parties. Keg registration provisions usually include disincentives for lying or not returning the keg, such as a large deposit, a tag on the keg with identifying information, and so forth.

The task force should first explore whether your community has a keg registration policy. If there is one, check to see if the provisions are consistent with model policies. If not, create one. Keg ordinances need to be written so that the industry can't skirt them. For example, when ordinances describe a keg as eight gallons, the industry may begin supplying "kegs" that are only 7.75 gallons. Try to design a policy that anticipates tactics the industry may use to get around the policy's intent.

Good keg registration information and advocacy can be found at the following websites:

- www.epi.umn.edu/alcohol/policy/img/SOCIAL _COMBINED_2005.PDF
- www.ncaddnj.org/file.axd?file=2010%2f11%2fKeg +Registration.pdf
- www.alcoholpolicy.niaaa.nih.gov/Keg_Registration.html

A model keg registration has been included in document 8 on the CD-ROM.[64]

Reducing Number of Physical Outlets

A high density of alcohol outlets is associated with heavy drinking. In college communities, many alcohol outlets compete by lowering price and selling higher volume (more on price issues in chapter 7). This is a chicken-and-egg phenomenon. There are lots of outlets because college students are a great market for alcohol. And the prevalence of outlets encourages students to binge-drink by making large volumes of alcohol readily available for low cost. This sends a message of community tolerance. The issue from your standpoint is not where to place blame but how to disrupt the current system.

Alcohol establishments have high turnover rates, especially those that cater to youth by selling high volumes of cheap alcohol. Though the bars turn over, the spaces get used for alcohol retail again and again, even as the owners change. However, the new ownership provides opportunities for intervention, and this is when the community can step in to reduce the number of licenses or upgrade the standards for service and their enforcement by placing specific conditions on liquor licenses.

Limiting Licenses

The National Institute on Alcohol Abuse and Alcoholism (NIAAA) recommends addressing the outlet density by limiting the number of licenses in the local community. Limiting the number of licenses available is one of the best options open to the community. What often happens is that the community, in the name of economic development, releases a new liquor license. The alcohol task force needs to be aware of this phenomenon and try to stop it through pressure on the city council and the people who enforce the license conditions. The local neighborhood association and possibly even the chamber of commerce may be helpful in this effort.

Limiting licenses is the first part of reducing physical access. The second part is to keep the density down via attrition. When an establishment goes out of business, encourage the community to forgo issuing a new license; help find a different business to fill the space. The limitations on licenses are usually supported by other license holders, because their license becomes more valuable as the availability shrinks.

Implementing the "Local Option"

Some states restrict localities from creating laws stricter than those at the state level. Exceptions to such restrictions are called "local option," "local control," or "preemption." This allows for a stricter ordinance. Though not strictly an alcohol policy, a local option can be an important part of controlling alcohol use in and near the campus.

Steady, predictable policy, enforcement, and deterrence are effective strategies to reshape a severe, deeply entrenched culture of binge drinking. In some cases, state laws are already sufficiently restrictive; they simply have not been enforced publicly and predictably. In such cases, the coalition should focus its effort on advocating for fair and consistent enforcement. However, sometimes the issue is that statewide laws are sufficient for most of the state—but too lax for the conditions in the community surrounding the campus. The coalition should then seek a "local option" to allow a stricter ordinance. Such options will require legislative action, so first check to see if the option already exists to enact local restrictions. A community that lacks local option will need to start by seeking this authority through state legislation. The case for the local option can be made by stating the *benefits* of your ultimate goal— the improvements in community and student well-being, creating an environment that reduces accidents, assaults, and other damages and promotes public health benefits; the savings in public resources; and so forth. As that goal is embraced, pair it with the reality that you cannot deliver those benefits without greater restrictions than those in place for the rest of the state. Note that the level of restrictions may be appropriate for the state (you are not asking for major change), but that your local situation requires an exception. Create a local option that can be realistically supported by the local legislative representatives. If the local-option argument is not making progress because state legislators want uniform standards throughout the state, the argument can still set the stage for pursuing tighter restrictions at the state level.[65]

Useful resources on local control:

- www.epi.umn.edu/alcohol/sample/framewrk.shtm
- www.alcoholpolicymd.com/pdf/Policy_Perils.pdf

CAsE EXAMPLE

FINDING OPPORTUNITIES FOR ADVOCACY

The Union Bar, a predominantly college student bar in Iowa City, Iowa, sponsored a series of bikini contests offering contestants prizes of up to $3,000. The local paper did a series of editorials about the potential risks. A month later, the state attorney general's office and the Iowa Alcoholic Beverages Division (ABD) filed a five-count complaint against the Union Bar. Charges included indecent exposure, dispensing alcohol to intoxicated persons, and providing alcohol to a minor. Eventually, the county attorney refused to sign the bar owner's application to renew the license for the bar, and then the city council denied the application as well. This was the first such denial in Iowa City in fifteen years. The media praised the city councilors who voted against the license.

The case for license renewal went to appeal. An administrative judge overturned the city council decision and granted the license. Other issues arose, though, of the bar's being out of compliance with Iowa City ordinances, which put the decision in the hands of the ABD administrator. The local binge-drinking prevention coalition at the University of Iowa, called "Stepping Up," supported efforts by the administrator to restrict features of the renewed

continued on next page

license. In the end the bar was suspended from operation for three weeks and had to pay a $2,000 fine.

There are some important lessons from this. First, the negative publicity and negative consequences (which included suspension, a fine, and potential jail time) sent a message to other bar owners in the neighborhood. Second, the people who enforce policy (the city council and ABD administrator) took action—with pressure from the community—in a way that they had not for some years. And, finally, community members interested in reducing the strong pattern of binge drinking and its negative impact on the community found out that they could make things happen. The alcohol coalition showed that local regulations mattered and could be enforced, and that the coalition could play a critical role in facilitating adherence to established community standards.[66]

Enforcing Laws and Regulations

The tactics described above rely on good enforcement. Enforcement, strategy 4, has a direct impact and a deterrent impact. It usually intervenes in the current practice—and the public awareness of consequences discourages future events. Here are some useful enforcement actions:

- Conduct targeted joint party patrol between campus and local police in the student neighborhoods surrounding campus.
- Work with the state or local alcohol beverage control agency.

- Hold establishments with alcohol licenses accountable.
- Design regulations and policies to include monitoring and enforcement.
- Check for compliance with regulations.
- Enforce false identification laws.
- Conduct DUI roadside checks.
- Target drinking hotspots.
- Adequately fund monitoring and enforcement.
- Enforce through insurance liability.

Conducting Targeted Joint Party Patrol

One effective enforcement strategy is a *party patrol,* where police conduct visible enforcement efforts both proactively and in response to neighborhood complaints. Campus and community police can conduct these patrols as joint operations, which can also help foster positive working relationships. This tactic can be conducted during anticipated heavy-drinking events, such as the first weekend of school, Halloween, or after sporting events. For example, as students arrive on the first weekend of school at the University of Nebraska–Lincoln, there's a forceful police presence in student neighborhoods where parties are known to occur. Squad cars, mounted police, and other symbols send a clear message that laws will be enforced. The violations enforced can include public consumption, minor in possession, disorderly house, noise disturbance, selling alcohol without a license, and assault. Check your local laws to find out what can be enforced. Enforcement efforts early in the school year can set the tone for deterrence and compliance with community standards.[67]

Colleges can use policy education strategies to inform students about the characteristics of parties that will be targeted for enforcement. This education, in combination with enforcement, can help students avoid creating a problematic environment.

Working with the State or Local Alcohol Beverage Control Agency

Alcohol beverage control agencies are often referred to as "ABCs." (The formal names of such agencies vary by state.) Every state recognizes that alcohol is a unique commodity that needs special regulation because it is a potentially dangerous product. Licensing is a part of this. Licensees need to meet various conditions, which vary by state/locality. The ABC helps enforce these conditions. Often the conditions are not carefully monitored for a variety of reasons. Colleges can learn what the ABC license requirements are and then work with the agencies to help them monitor the conditions in the public interest.

ABCs are chronically understaffed and under-resourced. Some work closely with local law enforcement, and others do not. Keep in mind that ABC authorities are sometimes political appointees and may not have a complete understanding of their important role. ABCs may underuse their own authority. Sometimes they don't feel politically supported in their ability to use their authority. In our experience, most ABCs would welcome the interest and support of colleges in getting their work done. (See, for example, the case example Finding Opportunities for Advocacy on page 141.)

Holding Establishments with Alcohol Licenses Accountable

Colleges can hold license holders to an agreed-upon set of community standards for good practices, including

- no sales to underage people (a law in all fifty states)
- no service to intoxicated individuals (nearly every state prohibits this, but the legal provisions vary by state)[68]
- adoption of dram shop laws with strict penalties

Keep in mind that the economic incentive for licensees is to *sell* alcohol. This can influence servers and sellers to look the other way regarding service to underage or to intoxicated people on occasion. And if one establishment persists in disregarding these standards as others try to comply, the economic benefit goes to the establishment that ignores the rule—students will flock to the establishment willing to serve underage and intoxicated people.

The alcohol task force, then, needs to find ways to hold the establishments to the regulations, which are an expression of the standards the community aspires to uphold. Though these efforts will meet with resistance, it benefits students, it benefits local businesses that have been harmed by the consequences of student drinking, and it benefits the bar owners who want to be good community citizens by providing a level playing field—they no longer are forced to compete by ignoring the rules.

So, find out what the license standards are in your area and hold licensees to those standards. Map alcohol outlets and match them with the number of service calls to police, ambulance, and fire. Anecdotally, the police already know where the trouble spots are, but your data will help provide evidence. Hard data of this sort make the relations obvious and weaken the arguments of those who don't want to comply. Targeted enforcement at these establishments can help raise the standards for the entire community.

Here are steps you can take:

- Understand *where* your students are running into problems. Systematically document which establishments are selling to students. When students wind up in detox, find out where they drank and where they were picked up.
- Work with campus and local police to get solid data, including the place of last drink for all DUI and other alcohol-related arrests.
- Use your relationship with the alcohol beverage control agencies to help them perform their public duty, which is to enforce the agreed-upon community standards.

College and university officials may be reluctant to get involved in what appears to be business and political issues surrounding the campus. But these issues directly affect the health, well-being, and academic success of their students. The administration, with the support and leadership of the task force, needs to work with the establishments to eliminate practices that encourage binge drinking. The college, through its community and political connections and its connections with local law enforcement, can make the case that it needs local help reducing the problems caused by student alcohol consumption. These partnerships can make everyone's job easier.

Designing Regulations and Policies to Include Monitoring and Enforcement

Compliance checks can be done not only at commercial establishments but also at the college among Greek houses and parties. A good policy regarding school-affiliated organizations will include the ability to monitor and check whether performance is matching the standard set in the policy—that is, a method of checking and enforcing compliance. (An example of standards in place at the University of Minnesota is described in the sidebar Risk Management at Greek Organizations, on pages 130–31.) Monitoring doesn't always have to be conducted by police. Self-monitoring and reporting can be effective and complement formal policing efforts, but these efforts should not replace or exclude monitoring by police. Awareness of existing city and state ordinances should also enable monitoring and enforcement.

Checking for Compliance with Regulations

Compliance checks on underage sales and sales to intoxicated people are effective at reducing access and maintaining community standards for serving alcohol in commercial establishments. Such checks can be done at commercial establishments, as well as at campus parties. Compliance checks can directly reduce noncompliance while having a deterrent effect, for example, by reducing the likelihood that servers will provide alcohol to underage or intoxicated individuals. Compliance checks may be conducted by the alcohol beverage control agency, the police, or other law enforcement agency. Alcohol coalitions that want to use this tactic should first review local laws to determine what is possible and then work with appropriate enforcement agencies to secure the necessary resources to do a good job. Grants for enforcement may be available through the U.S. Department of Justice. If the college has a death or other notable consequence related to alcohol on campus, the tragedy can provide the impetus to move state legislators to release more resources for enforcement of standards.

Good protocols are available for underage and over-service compliance checks by law enforcement (see the website of the Office of Juvenile Justice and Delinquency Prevention at www.ojjdp.gov). Schools can encourage enforcement of policies at Greek parties, other affiliated organizations, college housing, and rental housing. However, sometimes these organizations will resist until they are caught or experience a major negative consequence, such as a death or sexual assault. The consequences they face serve as a deterrent for others.

Most schools have access to good survey tools, and these can be used to gather anonymous, aggregate data on underage drinking and intoxication. These tools can be used to help the coalition determine where and how to target their enforcement efforts.

A manual for conducting compliance checks is online at www.epi .umn.edu/alcohol/manual/index.shtm. Background on compliance checks can be found at www.epi.umn.edu/alcohol/policy/compchks.shtm.

Enforcing False Identification Laws

Underage drinkers are adept at creating false identification cards, and the Internet provides many options for a student to purchase a fake ID. Stepped-up enforcement (and public examples of it) can act as a deterrent. Changes in the types of identification issued by the state can also help. (The time to press for improvements in identification is when state identifications specs are being revisited.)

Learn more about the enforcement of false ID laws at www.pire.org
/documents/FalseIdentification.pdf.

Conducting DUI Roadside Checks

Roadside checks for DUI have similar impact as compliance checks for
other alcohol restrictions—deterrence and reduction of incidence.
Many states run regular roadside checks or post notices that checks
will be run during heavy-drinking times. These tend to be concentrated in areas where there is a high incidence of problems and also in
jurisdictions where local authorities want to (or prioritize resources to)
implement them. Roadside checks could be focused near campus before
and after major events that likely involve heavy drinking, such as sporting events. If the campus is having a particular problem, a big show of
compliance checkpoints goes a long way to diminishing future use.
Checks could be done outside bars or at roadside stops at main arterials
near campus. The advantage of a big public display is that, if done once
at the beginning of the year, there is a strong carryover effect; people
remember it and think law enforcement is doing it all the time, so they
are more careful. Such checks work on the demand-side of alcohol. They
make negative consequences visible and probable, and so people choose
other entertainment options.

Targeting Drinking Hotspots

The college can target enforcement efforts at large drinking parties,
where negative consequences (such as physical or sexual assault)
occur. The alcohol coalition can start by gathering data on alcohol
incident reports, look at how they tend to cluster, and predict where
such parties will happen in the future. Although this strategy may not
entirely eliminate neighborhood parties, targeting drinking hotspots
can successfully and rapidly shrink a party from four hundred guests
to perhaps a dozen. True, the remaining dozen may still drink, and
some of the other scattered students may as well, but overall fewer will

drink, and they will drink less. Thus, you will lower the risks associated with having a large, concentrated group of people who are intoxicated. Success is measured by reducing the size of the problem, not by its total elimination. Changing a party from a mob to a handful is a win. The targeted intervention also deters future gatherings and shrinks their size. Publicizing the enforcement can remind potential party hosts of the negative consequences.

Besides house and fraternity parties, the college and local law enforcement can target events, whether big game days, college festivals, or other traditions. Enforcement does not have to be all negative: you can also reinforce and teach the importance of good service practices, the presence of a sober monitor, and the use of professional bartenders who are trained to serve alcohol and monitor intoxicants. Enforcement may also include pat-downs for alcohol at the entry doors of sporting events and parties, and sobriety monitors who look for the entrance of people who appear to be intoxicated.

Adequately Funding Monitoring and Enforcement

Compliance checks and prosecution can be time consuming and expensive. Police are reluctant to intervene in activities when they know there is not going to be good follow-through in the judicial system, or when they have limited resources and may feel the time and money is better spent on other enforcement problems (theft, battery, etc.). These same objections are frequently raised by groups *opposing* new policies, such as students and the alcohol industry. Enforcement that appears lax may have to do with resource availability. The college can lobby for more resources and more efficient use of existing resources for enforcement. If there are only two patrol cars and six police in a college town, the police cannot possibly deal with the needs in the town. Colleges can lobby for more money and officers. They can also, if they have their own police or security force, add staff of their own and make a show of enforcement in partnership with local law enforcement. Local neighborhood associations and chambers of commerce can be allies in seeking funding for increased enforcement.

The presence of police—as in the example of opening day at the University of Nebraska–Lincoln—sends a clear message that enforcement *may* happen. But the enforcers should actually be visibly enforcing. The mechanism through which this works is by increasing the perceived likelihood of being caught and held accountable. This can be dealt with through lobbying, resources, and public pressure.

Enforcement pressure can also be applied through media advocacy. Let reporters know about the events going on in bars and the damages that follow. For example, the flaming shots offered by a bar got out of control, spilled, and set the bar on fire; the negative attention in the newspaper eventually led to the bar being shut down.

Enforcing through Insurance Liability

Legal enforcement is not the only form of enforcement open to the college. Insurance liability risks are borne by those who serve alcohol. Colleges can work with fraternity houses (and with their national organizations) to understand and mitigate the potential insurance liability they face. Practices that reduce the risk for service to underage or intoxicated guests and patrons are good risk management as well. Organizations may be highly motivated by reducing their liability.

COALITION SUCCEEDS THROUGH POLICY, LEGISLATION, AND ENFORCEMENT[69]

A project in Atlanta to reduce campus binge drinking is a good example of the use of policy, existing laws, new laws, enforcement and improved enforcement funding, public education, collaboration, and media advocacy. The Georgia Tech GT SMART campus-community coalition had excellent success with community policies in the Greater Atlanta area. Key partnerships helped the coalition achieve its mission.

One notable example was with the Atlanta Police Department (APD) to foster police involvement and to develop a partnership plan. Primarily the goal was to reduce opportunities for underage and high-risk drinking through increased enforcement of ordinances, monitoring of alcohol licensees, community awareness and participation, and encouraging more citizen calls to 9-1-1 (the community emergency phone number). To accomplish this, GT SMART anticipated needs of the APD that would prevent police cooperation. The project identified a grant that enabled the police department to add patrol officers on evening shifts. Extra staff facilitated a 38 percent increase in alcohol violation citations from 2004 to 2006. The APD also initiated a deputy program that trained civilian employees to augment sworn officers in the field in conducting alcohol compliance checks on alcohol licensed businesses and issuing citations to businesses in violation of the code.

Other collaborations led to passage of state and municipal alcohol control legislation. GT SMART supported the statewide Georgia Alcohol Policy Partnership in successfully advocating for passage of legislation to require registration of beer kegs whereby

continued on next page

alcohol vendors are more easily held responsible for selling kegs to underage patrons. A record of each keg purchaser is kept to expedite the process of tracking the sources of underage drinking. Georgia law requires anyone buying a keg to sign an affidavit listing the location where the keg is to be consumed and acknowledging that it is illegal to furnish alcohol to minors.

In partnership with community leaders and city officials, GT SMART assisted in drafting eleven separate pieces of legislation that were adopted by the Atlanta City Council, including reduction of beverage sales hours, zoning changes limiting the density of alcohol sales outlets, increased enforcement, and a revised alcohol sales permit application process.

Police need citizen cooperation to uncover illegal activities. GT SMART, in a partnership with the APD, established an anonymous tip line at Georgia Tech for the public to provide information about Atlanta bars, restaurants, and stores suspected of selling or serving alcohol to underage or intoxicated persons. Announced at several press conferences covered by local press and National Public Radio, the Anonymous Tip Hotline became a safe and effective method for concerned citizens to report suspected alcohol license violations to law enforcement agencies. Refrigerator magnets with the tip line phone number were distributed at community meetings, at neighborhood events, and by mail to residents of Atlanta.

The coalition also paid constant attention to public attitudes and concerns. GT SMART used an opinion research firm to survey Atlanta residents to assess whether high-risk drinking and its secondhand effects were impacting quality of life and to gauge support for potential policy changes. Information gained was used to adjust approaches in community meetings.

Helpful Resources

We recommend you review the publication *Strategies to Reduce Underage Alcohol Use,* written by Kathryn Stewart and staff of the Pacific Institute for Research and Evaluation (PIRE) for the Office of Juvenile Justice and Delinquency Prevention (OJJDP). The document is available online at www.udetc.org/documents /strategies.pdf. The section Strategies Aimed at Reducing Social Availability of Alcohol reinforces many of our recommendations, including keg registration laws and increased enforcement, and contains helpful case examples.

Media advocacy is a critical portion of your work, and is especially helpful when seeking to increase enforcement resources and activity or when working with policy makers to beef up regulations. *Strategic Media Advocacy for Enforcement of Underage Drinking Laws,* also prepared for OJJDP by the Pacific Institute, may be downloaded at www.udetc.org /documents/mediaadvocacy.pdf. The document discusses basics such as message framing, creating media bites, and dealing with journalists. It was developed prior to the onset of social media, and so does not cover its uses, but those resources create additional opportunities to advocate for positive change. As a basic primer, it is quite helpful.

Chapter Summary

The two most effective strategies a college can pursue to reduce alcohol consumption among its students are to restrict access to alcohol and to increase its price. This chapter focused on two key strategies that restrict access: creating or improving policies that reduce the physical and social availability of alcohol and enforcing (or implementing) regulations. Many of these actions can be taken on campus and in the nearby community, but they require the cooperation and action of other local groups—neighborhood associations, city council members, the legal system, the local alcohol beverage control agency, health care providers, and many others. As your task force works on these strategies, it will gain success by ensuring that it finds and enlists local and regional allies who have clout or who know how to push the buttons of those people who do. Local and regional media can help you bring issues to greater awareness and apply appropriate pressure to improve the life of your students and your neighbors.

In the next chapter, we'll look at the second critical strategy: raising the price of alcohol.

CHAPTER 7

INFLUENCING ALCOHOL PRICES

The price of alcohol and drinking behavior are importantly related—and sometimes the link can be deadly. Mankato, Minnesota, is home to a state university. It's a midsized college sixty-five miles south of Minneapolis, serving about fifteen thousand undergraduate and graduate students each year. Early in the fall semester of 2007, a twenty-one-year-old woman who had attended the school died of alcohol poisoning.

Hers was one of four alcohol-related deaths of college-aged youth in Mankato during the semester. Binge drinking was the likely cause of the death of two college-aged men in North Mankato, and alcohol poisoning killed another female student in Mankato.

It took the loss of four lives to get a new city ordinance into place—one that would ban limitless drinking specials. The ban had been debated for months; earlier enactment may have saved some lives.[70]

Binge drinking is the cheapest form of entertainment in most college towns. Raising the price of alcohol near campus, including the elimination of drink discount promotions, may be the single-most effective policy-based strategy to reduce binge drinking.

A systematic review conducted by the United States Preventive Services Task Force of all available studies of the impact of alcohol prices showed that higher alcohol prices or taxes were consistently related to

- fewer motor vehicle crashes and fatalities (ten of eleven studies)

- less alcohol-impaired driving (three of three studies)
- less mortality from liver cirrhosis (five of five studies)
- less all-cause mortality (one study)

Effects also were demonstrated for measures of violence (three studies), sexually transmitted diseases (one study), and alcohol dependence (one study).[71]

The drinking behavior of most college students is very sensitive to the price of alcohol. Although students are likely to argue that their behavior would not change if new taxes were implemented or price discounting were eliminated, a large number of studies tell the opposite story. In fact, students may argue against pursuing policies that raise the price of alcohol while at the same time denying it would influence their own behavior, perhaps because such policies are effective.

Students are looking for entertainment and a way to facilitate social relationships among their fellow students, most of whom are in completely new social settings. Alcohol is a low-cost solution for both of these issues. If you doubt this, put yourself in the shoes of a college student and do some price comparisons.

TABLE 7.1

Cost of Alcohol versus Other Entertainment Options

ACTIVITY	COST/PERSON
Two shots of vodka (social consumption)	$1.18
Five shots of vodka (binge to intoxication)	$2.95
Two servings of beer (social consumption)	$1.12
Five servings of beer (binge to intoxication)	$2.79
First-run movie	$12.00
Medium coffee at coffee shop	$2.95
Fast food meal of hamburger, fries, and soft drink	$4.99

As a student, you (or an older friend) can get a fifth of bottom-shelf vodka for $10. That bottle will yield about seventeen shots. Table 7.1 shows how that stacks up against some other entertainment options.

You can see that getting drunk is cheap entertainment. You think it will be fun, though you may risk feeling bad afterward; you think it will ease socially awkward conditions; and you can more easily afford it.

Of course, many of the consequences of drinking to excess may prove to be negative and expensive—consequences *not* shared by the other entertainment options. But you are young. Like most young people, you lack the experience to imagine consequences. And so you choose to binge-drink.

Even when young people are aware of consequences, they tend to think, *Consequences are what happen to someone else.* This is not mature thinking—but then, these are not fully mature thinkers. Older people tend to forget this simple difference. Lack of money, social vulnerability, and poor judgment help explain why college students choose excessive drinking.

A large number of studies have demonstrated that alcohol consumption is strongly influenced by price. In fact, an analysis of 112 studies of alcohol tax or price conducted in 2009 showed a very strong association between price (or tax) and consumption—the higher the price, the lower the consumption.[72] The literature review suggests that increasing the cost of alcohol has a large impact compared to other alcohol prevention policies and programs.

This is why raising the price of alcohol near campus is a critical strategy for your group. In this chapter, we suggest two tactics that will support these efforts.

Tactic 1. Reduce or eliminate price specials and other discounts.
Tactic 2. Raise prices through taxation.

For both of these tactics, you can begin by gathering data.

Gather Price Data

The coalition needs to start by gathering facts for the local region. These facts will help sharpen your ability to be effective with both tactics above. Do the research on prices in your community and fill out table 7.2. You can add other popular entertainment choices.

TABLE 7.2

Alcohol and Entertainment Price Data

Use this or a similar table to gather data on the costs of entertainment options students consider. In developing the table, add in the variety of forms of alcohol known to be popular with students on your campus. Also add other forms of nearby entertainment alternatives that are likely to appeal to students.

ACTIVITY	COST/PERSON
Two shots (cheap bottle of spirits)	
Five shots (cheap bottle of spirits)	
Beer/drink purchased in keg quantities	
Wine (cheap bottle)	
Beer (local bars)	
Spirit drinks (local bars)	
Wine (local bar)	
First-run movie	
Coffee at coffee shop (16 oz.)	
Fast food meal (hamburger, fries, and soft drink)	
Buying and playing a video game	

A table like this helps educate your group about the comparative costs and the activities competing for students' disposable income. It is also compelling evidence for use with local community leaders. It tends to wake up the mayor, town council members, and the press to the cost of alcohol relative to other options.

In addition to this basic pricing information, we encourage you to gather data on the drink discounts and specials going on in the community around your campus. These can be found in the local entertainment weekly, possibly in the school paper (depending on the school's advertising policy), in other postings around the campus, at the bars themselves, and in the local paper. Students at the college are your best data collectors for this kind of information. (The sidebar What to Include in an Alcohol Tax Fact Sheet, page 175, has ideas for other data you could collect, which will be useful as you fight pricing discounts or seek to raise alcohol excise taxes.)

Also gather advertisements and photograph on-site specials—two-for-one ads, ladies-drink-free nights, bottomless-cup ads, and so forth. Seek out news clippings on local incidents related to youth drinking during such specials, and develop a file. All this information can become part of a PowerPoint presentation to the people you are trying to persuade. Figure 7.1 shows some of the ads we've collected over time.

FIGURE 7.1

Sample Ads for Drink Specials

Wednesday: Live Music at 10pm!
$3 Pitchers of Buffalo Wings
(8pm-Close)
2-for-1's on Anything Behind
the Bar (8pm-Close)

Thursday: Karaoke with
Ick at 10pm!
$2 Coors Lights
$2.50 Long Islands

Saturday: DJ Kazaam!
$12 Buckets of Beer (12pm-6pm)
$3 You Call It Shots (9pm-12am)
$3 Domestic Bottles (9pm to close)

DRINKING GAME: Sloppy Sixes

With all the perverted and imaginative minds here at _____ it's pretty easy to get carried away with wild drinking games. But don't get us wrong, we still like classics, quick and easy, just like the way we like our women. Just to prove it to you, we're keeping this week's game simple, like your cousin Alvin.

What You'll Need: Any alcohol hiding in the back of your cabinet and some dice.
Number of Players: As many cool guys as you can get your hands on.
Intoxication Level: We'll make ya extra schloppy!

Let's Get Sloppy:
- Line up three cups and three shot glasses, numbering them from one to six.
- Fill them up with anything that will get you drunk: beer, whisky, nail polish remover, whatever floats your boat.
- Take turns flipping a die. The number you roll is the drink you take.
- Do not fill up the glass after drinking from it.
- When a player rolls a six, they may give that drink out to another player.
- If a cup is empty and you roll its number, you miss your turn and have to fill up the cup instead. Don't be discouraged, though, you'll be happy for this break later.

The Game Ends When: Either the alcohol runs out or someone yacks. Bon appa-drinking!

Thirsty for More?

In combination, the price comparison and ad presentation will capture the attention of key stakeholders. This information can be very effective in showing that *something* must be done to raise the price of entry to drinking.

With your data in hand, you can begin working on price changes. The first tactic is to work on eliminating the specials and discounts that effectively reduce the price of drinking.

Tactic 1: Reduce or Eliminate Discounts.

Your work to reduce or eliminate discounts and other pricing specials involves a series of steps.

1. Understand How Wholesalers and Leading Outlets Organize

Alcohol wholesalers and retailers will likely organize to fight back against your efforts to change pricing. They may try to combat your efforts completely. If this fails, they may try to co-opt your efforts by adopting "voluntary" restrictions. These almost never work to reduce price or heavy drinking; they have no teeth and may last a short period of time at most, falling apart the minute one bar fails to comply. Be careful—if you agree to ineffective voluntary restrictions, you may damage the credibility of your task force. The retailers who are working against your efforts may point to the voluntary agreement as an example of failure, and suggest that further efforts aren't worth the time. Make sure that voluntary agreements have provisions for mandatory restrictions if the voluntary agreements fail.

2. Find Allies in the Alcohol Industry

You will be able to find allies out there. Many retailers want to operate their businesses in a responsible way and recognize that irresponsible alcohol consumption is linked to problems in the community, that binge drinking puts young people and others at risk, and that the elimination of alcohol-focused price reductions can reduce some of those problems. All of these things can place their businesses at risk. Find the retailers who recognize this and are willing to stand up and promote the elimination of price discounting within reach of the campus (if not across the region). Allies are likely to be found among the establishments that also (or primarily) serve food. For them, selling alcohol at a higher price (and focusing on quality) can be a benefit. They grow weary of competing against retailers that typically focus more on volume than quality. Some of these quality establishments will speak publicly on the benefits of raising price. They'll also note that efforts to increase price will fail unless everyone works together. Better than anyone, they'll be able to argue *against* the voluntary restrictions and *for* some legal action to change low-price competition near campus.

3. Understand the Perspective of Alcohol Businesses

Bars and restaurants are in business. Their motivations are very different from those of the college and of the task force. Make it your business to learn about *their* business. You need to know how the changes you seek will impact them, their bottom lines, and their employees. Is there a way they can make money without contributing to the problem? Perhaps you can enlist faculty from the business, marketing/public relations, and economics departments to assist your efforts.

There are various ways of making money on alcohol. Some establishments compete on quality, and others compete on volume. College life, poor judgment, near-empty pockets, and the persistent drive for "fun" combine to make college students a target for the retailers who compete on volume—selling lots of the cheapest stuff at the lowest price. You need to understand this business model, because it is the model that continually drives some establishments toward steep discounts and other price cuts, while dragging along others who must discount to stay competitive. Meanwhile, your goal is to help create an environment that favors other beneficial behaviors (a good meal; good entertainment). Just remember that most alternatives can't compete against low-priced alcohol. So long as alcohol is available cheaply, it will out-compete almost any college-sponsored alcohol-free event. This is also a reason to work on outlet density issues (see our discussion of this issue in chapter 6) and reduce outlets through attrition by making sure those who operate in compliance with community standards for serving alcohol are the ones that survive, rather than the establishments that have risky business practices.

4. Take Specific Actions

Localities in and around campuses have had success with the following:

- If you have a pub on campus, institute a campus-wide no-discounts policy. This is a step in the right direction.
- Ban drink specials in the local environment. This approach is relatively straightforward when only one city is in play. However, when the school is near several towns with varied policies, a coordinated coalition effort is needed. Some businesses are skilled at pitting neighboring town councils against each other; be aware of this possibility and plan for it.
- Advocate at the regional and state levels to cease or reduce discounting practices. Band together with like-minded groups, such as other colleges and local prevention coalitions, to advocate at the broadest levels. This allows you to

coordinate contacts, ask for similar changes and uniform enforcement, and circumvent a race to the bottom if town councils compete to offer the most lax alcohol environment in an attempt to lure customers.

The ability to advocate at the local or regional level varies from state to state.[73] There are examples where it may be quite difficult. Take Florida, for instance. Florida is one of eleven states that lack statutes restricting drink specials, according to the Tampa Alcohol Coalition. In 2006, according to the *Tampa Tribune*, the Tampa city attorney asked the Florida attorney general for an opinion on the ability of a city or county to enact a drink-special ordinance; the attorney general said that cities can't adopt special ordinances in Florida.[74] This strategy was not feasible given state laws in Florida. Do a little digging and understand what is possible in your state or region. Work with your university attorneys, city attorneys, and law school professors, if applicable, to identify feasible strategies within the current legal environment in your community.

Even when you can't institute regulatory controls of price discount at the *local* level, you can use media campaigns, advocacy, and counter-advertising to apply community pressure on such establishments. Such campaigns have been found to be an important and effective component of enforcement efforts. Counter-advertising was effective against tobacco use, and the same tactic may also work to create better norms for alcohol use in the community.[75] This is an excellent activity in which student groups can engage. They may need some encouragement and an understanding of how advertising and promotion influence the drinking environment, but they can be terrific sources of creative ways of working on these issues.

The guide *How to Use Local Regulatory and Land Use Powers to Prevent Underage Drinking*, published by the Office of Juvenile Justice and Delinquency Prevention, has more information on tactics that can ultimately increase alcohol's price and decrease its availability. You may download a copy at www.udetc.org/documents/regulatory.pdf.

Sample Discounting Ordinance Language

Below are samples of ordinance language used to restrict alcohol discounts.[76]

Sample Restricting "Two-for-One" Deals

[I]t shall be unlawful for any licensee: To establish a single retail price based upon the required purchase of two or more drinks. *Alabama Admin. Code Supp. § 20-X-6.14(1)(b) (Sept. 1990)*

Sample Restricting Happy Hour Discounts

It is unlawful for a holder of a retailer's permit to: Sell alcoholic beverages during a portion of the day at a price that is reduced from the . . . established price that the permittee charges during the remainder of that day. *Indiana Stat. Ann. § 7.1-5-10-20(a)(1) (1991)*

Sample Restricting Volume Discounts

The holder of a permit issued by the department of liquor control . . . shall not: Increase the volume of alcoholic beverages contained in a serving without increasing proportionately the price charged for such serving. *Ohio Admin. Code § 4301:1-1-50 (3) (1994)*

Sample Restricting "All You Can Drink" Discounts

On premises where alcoholic beverages are sold by the drink, a licensee . . . may not sell . . . an unlimited number of alcoholic beverages . . . during a set period of time for a fixed price. *Alaska Statutes § 04.16.015(a)(4) (Oct. 1994)*

continued on next page

Sample Restricting "Ladies Drink Free" Deals

An on-premise permittee . . . shall not give away a drink or sell one at a price that is different from the usual . . . price charged for the drink for any period of time less than one full business day. Free or reduced drinks under this provision shall be offered to all customers, not just a segment of the population. *North Carolina Admin. Code § 4.2S.0232(b) (1994)*

5. Practice Patience and Pressure

The alcohol task force has two important assets: patience and pressure. Work with town leaders and members of the business community to set positive business standards that are incompatible with the high-volume, low-price model. Monitoring and enforcing community standards on alcohol establishments can help push the volume-based establishments out of town or out of business. Time is on your side. Many high-volume, cheap-drink bars will flame out quickly; it's important to step up enforcement (discussed in chapter 6) to keep new licenses from going out to new cheap-booze retailers. In this game, winning is not about getting one place closed. It's about maintaining constant pressure over the long haul while the culture changes. And it's about helping all establishments learn that staying in business means complying with community standards for good service practices.

College towns may be reluctant to enforce the standards that put an end to deep discounting. And in some communities, the bar owners are politically savvy and have built long-term relationships with enforcement agents, political leaders, and others. Just keep in mind that the culture of heavy drinking, and the businesses that thrive on it, is deep-seated. The existing system incentivizes cheap, high-volume alcohol, lax enforcement, and tolerance of low standards. Keep the pressure on over the long haul, and the conditions that shape your culture will change.

Tactic 2: Raise Prices through Taxation.

Raising alcohol prices via taxation is considered highly effective in reducing alcohol consumption and is a recommended tactic by the CDC and NIAAA.

However, this is the tactic colleges are *least likely* to take on. In our research with more than 350 colleges, less than 2 percent were pursuing this strategy.[77] Why? A major challenge to getting these policies enacted is that college administrators who work on alcohol issues don't believe it is within their purview to change local or state policy. Of course, colleges cannot change community policy directly, but they can have a major influence on it if they try. State-level advocacy effort is difficult. Also, it can be risky for state-system colleges to go out on a limb in front of the same legislators who fund them. Yet this tactic is effective when implemented, and worth the time and effort. Frame your alcohol control advocacy as a way to provide a safe, healthy environment that will maximize the investment the public already makes in higher education.

Federal alcohol taxes have not been raised in forty years. This means that alcohol taxes have effectively been dropping, since they do not automatically adjust for inflation. Few states have addressed taxes on alcohol. The most recent tax hike was in Maryland in 2011. This was not a huge increase—5 cents a gallon—and took considerable effort to achieve. But it is helping to reduce problems associated with alcohol and raising needed revenue that can cover some of the costs governments already pay to deal with community alcohol issues. Keep in mind that alcohol extracts huge costs on society—an estimated $220 billion in the United States annually, and most of that cost is covered by taxpayers—and on colleges specifically as discussed in chapter 1. Legislators usually resist raising revenue via alcohol excise taxes, and the political environment for taxation is difficult. Taxes may go into a general fund, into enforcement of alcohol regulations, into treatment, or for other uses such as schools and health care. The public is generally more likely to support an alcohol tax when the revenues are specifically directed to fund prevention and treatment programs, especially if they are already paying these costs through general taxation. Frame this issue as a way for drinkers to pay the hidden social costs they inflict on your community.

Don't Lose a State Monopoly

Eighteen U.S. states have monopoly control of alcohol sales. There has been a push for these states to privatize alcohol monopolies. This is a bad trend. Loss of monopoly removes a series of controls that ultimately influence price. Alcohol consumption tends to be more moderate when the state controls the retail sale through monopoly. States with such monopoly have a lower prevalence of drinking and binge drinking among people between the ages of twelve and twenty-five as compared to those that license private sellers. Privatization can lead to higher alcohol-outlet density, increased availability, and declines in price. When the beer sales monopoly was reinstated in Sweden, alcoholism, alcohol psychosis, and intoxication decreased by more than 20 percent among youth.[78] Plus, states that have recently

continued on next page

privatized have given away their monopoly for pennies on the dollar, turning a public resource that functions to protect public safety and generate significant annual revenue into private financial gain for a few people.

If your state has monopoly control, the alcohol coalition should keep an eye on it and protect it. Keep reinforcing the benefits of such control, and counter efforts to privatize.

More resources on this topic can be found at the following websites:

▸ *State Control of Alcohol: Protecting the Public's Health.* This fact sheet provides useful data on the benefits of monopoly control and the negative consequences of privatization. Download it at www.alcap.com/clientimages/39796/marin %20institutecontrolstates_factsheet.pdf.

▸ *Alcohol Control Systems: Retail Distribution Systems for Beer.* This Web page provides great detail on the laws addressing retail distribution of beer, including state-run, private licensed sellers, or combination systems. See it at www.alcoholpolicy.niaaa.nih.gov/Alcohol _Control_Systems_Retail_Distribution_Systems _for_Beer.html. (Note: This link relates to beer. There are pages in the system on beer, wine, and spirits, and for wholesale and retail.)

▸ The National Alcohol Beverage Control Association is a resource for control states and a potential partner for colleges interested in working on control policies. See www.nabca.org.

Advocates have dealt with tax resistance by qualifying alcohol taxes as a "fair share" of the social costs of alcohol. The arguments for this include the following:

- The costs of new excise taxes to moderate drinkers are relatively low. That is, if you have only one to three drinks, at $1 extra per drink, you have not experienced a big hit.
- Meanwhile, those who drink to excess pay more, and thus help to cover the social costs associated with their heavy drinking.
- It's unfair to force all taxpayers to subsidize the cost of problems created by a few heavy drinkers. The negative consequences heavy drinkers generate disproportionately impact health care costs, automobile insurance, and the costs of public safety. Currently taxpayers who do not drink or drink very little subsidize the costs of drinking for the heaviest drinkers. Taxes on alcohol are fair because they provide some revenues to cover those costs. They could be considered a "user fee."

This argument was successfully used in San Francisco to gain passage of a city fee ordinance called the "Charge for Harm" bill. The bill proposed charging alcohol wholesalers and others for some of the city's unreimbursed alcohol-related costs. It was supported by data in a study titled "The Cost of Alcohol to San Francisco." The bill passed the Board of Supervisors by a 6–3 vote in 2010, but was quickly vetoed by the mayor.[79]

The argument has validity and power. Recasting a tax as a *user fee* has been an effective strategy even among "no new taxes" politicians.[80] The primary talking point to reinforce this: alcohol taxes help recoup some of the social costs of drinking. These costs include increased nonviolent and violent crime, accidents, property damage, and health consequences, the costs of which come out of the taxpayers' pockets.

Opponents will respond to this by saying that a tax on all drinkers is unfair. A typical argument is, "Why does my one glass of chardonnay have to support problems caused by drunken college students?"

The response is to reinforce the user fee aspect of the tax: the vast majority of the tax will be paid by the heavy drinkers. Though your glass of chardonnay may cost you one dollar more, heavy drinkers will be paying five to eight dollars more for their night of binge drinking. A study that examined the impact of a hypothetical national 25-cent tax found that higher-risk drinkers would pay nearly five times more than lower-risk drinkers and 82.7 percent of increased taxes overall. Lower-risk drinkers would pay less than thirty dollars in net increased taxes annually.[81] Other optional activities have costs associated with them, and those who participate in the optional activities are usually required to pay for those extra costs associated with them—it's not unlike selling fishing licenses to help cover the costs of fishery maintenance in the state.

Equally important, the higher price may push those who binge to drink less. As they consume less, the reality is that they do less damage. That reduces costs for everyone.

Finally, the increase in price can send the message that the community condones moderate, healthy choices and condemns reckless behavior.

This framing helps present the excise tax or user fee as an issue of fairness and positive community standards, which makes it more palatable among those generally opposed to taxation.

Research supports this view. A study of the economic costs and benefits of alcohol taxation showed that an alcohol tax of 20 percent of the pre-tax retail price resulted in net cost savings to the community. These savings were in the form of decreased community costs for police and emergency services, health care, counseling and intervention, and lost productivity. Another study looked at "disability-adjusted life-years," which express time lost to premature death and to disability by disease or accident. Studies of the economic efficiency of

increasing taxes show that a modest initial investment to get the legislation passed, plus the cost of administering and enforcing the laws, results
in either overall cost savings or very small costs for each prevented
death or disability. In other words, taxing alcohol is a great investment
in prevention.[82]

Implementing higher alcohol taxes will save the community money,
bring in new revenues, and improve community standards. If colleges
take leadership in this effort, they are helping the community. For many
institutions, this aligns very naturally with the college mission statement, as well as the budget—since reduced alcohol-related damage saves
the campus money.

The basic advocacy steps are simple to state, but, of course, implementation is difficult. Here are the steps:

1. Understand the political and cultural environment.

2. Develop compelling facts and statistics, but relay them
   in terms of personal stories. (The sidebar What to
   Include in an Alcohol Tax Fact Sheet on page 175 has
   helpful suggestions.)

3. Make your arguments relevant to the locale and to the
   people you are seeking to persuade.

4. Frame your arguments to show the benefits of the change
   you are advocating. People seek to avoid losses more than
   they seek to achieve gains, so emphasize the savings for the
   community rather than the costs. Show the benefits to
   retailers as well, in terms of a more even playing field,
   lower business costs (e.g., reduced vandalism and liability),
   and improved community reputation. Compare the
   future benefits the regulatory change will bring to the
   costs of the status quo.

5. Test your arguments and prepare for the counter-
   arguments. Prepare to deal with the alcohol industry
   (see the subsequent section in this chapter).

6. Tally the college's own costs of dealing with alcohol problems on campus. For example, note the number of person-hours spent reacting to student drinking problems, the requisite contacts, discipline, follow-up, enforcement of penalties, repairs to property destruction, costs of added insurance, and so forth. Show the expenses. Use them in your argument. Then relate the college costs to the costs in the greater community. Show how this is a winning change for the community, for those who fund the college (it reduces campus costs—especially important for public institutions), and so forth.

7. Find allies across the region and state and align your arguments. Share networks and contacts, and use your leverage with local policy makers.

8. Keep the issue in front of the decision makers. The drinking culture will not change overnight. It will take years of effort, and you need to keep the pressure on. Continually collect and present current facts about your local situation and keep getting them out to power brokers. The more specific your information is to your local situation, the more powerful the impact.

Sample Alcohol Excise Tax Language

Sample alcohol excise tax language can be found by looking at Maryland's recent bill. We've excerpted it below.

SENATE BILL 717 (excerpt)

page 4, lines 4–18

(a) Except as provided in subsection (d) of this section, the alcoholic beverage tax rate for distilled spirits is:

(1) [$1.50] **$10.03** for each gallon or [39.63 cents] **$2.65** for each liter; and

(2) if distilled spirits contain a percentage of alcohol greater than 100 proof, an additional tax, for each 1 proof over 100 proof, of [1.5] **10.03** cents for each gallon or [0.3963] **2.65** cents for each liter.

(b) Except as provided in subsection (d) of this section, the alcoholic beverage tax rate for wine is [40 cents] $2.96 for each gallon or [10.57] **78.22** cents for each liter.

(c) Except as provided in subsection (d) of this section, the alcoholic beverage tax rate on beer is [9 cents] **$1.16** for each gallon or [2.3778] **30.6472** cents for each liter.

(d) The tax imposed under § 5–102(b) of this subtitle shall equal the amount that the discriminating jurisdiction charges a Maryland licensee or permit holder.

　　The entire bill may be viewed at http://mlis.state.md .us/2010rs/bills/sb/sb0717f.pdf.

　　For more information on Maryland's efforts to increase the state's alcohol tax, see http://cspinet .org/booze/taxguide/TaxMDPrint.htm.

What to Include in an Alcohol Tax Fact Sheet

In 2011, Maryland successfully passed a law raising alcohol taxes from 6 percent to 9 percent. The increase was expected to generate $85 million in its first year. Funds will go to programs for the disabled, to schools, and to school construction. The law is expected to save lives by reducing underage drinking and alcohol abuse. Advocates worked for years to pass the law; it was the first increase in wine and beer taxes since 1972, and the first in spirits taxes since 1955. To bolster their efforts, the tax proponents cited the benefits to health resulting from Maryland's increase in tobacco taxes in 1991, 2002, and 2007. Those increases are linked to 200,000 fewer smokers in 2011 than in 2001.[83]

A large coalition of groups supported passage of the bill, called the Lorraine Sheehan Health and Community Services Act of 2011. The fact sheets prepared by this coalition can be viewed at the website of Health Care for All (www.healthcareforall.com). The following are some of the facts the coalition used to support its cause. Your coalition could develop these facts for your state:

▶ amount of increase the tax would create per drink

▶ anticipated tax revenues

▶ suggested disbursement of the revenues

▶ savings in health care costs due to reductions

continued on next page

in alcohol abuse, reductions in aggravated assaults and rapes, reductions in violence against children, and reductions in premature deaths

▶ job preservation and creation in health care sector

▶ reductions in underage drinking

▶ your state's (or region's) current ranking in alcohol taxation nationwide

▶ change in share of budget paid for by alcohol excise topics

▶ polling data showing support for the proposal

▶ cost of increase to "non-risky" (moderate) drinkers (this amount is typically small)

▶ research on impact of border-crossing to purchase alcohol

▶ current death and violent crimes associated with alcohol use

▶ number and percent of high school and underage college drinkers

▶ alcohol-related deaths among underage drinkers

▶ annual costs of harmful alcohol use

Fact sheets should include the names of all the supporters or members of your alcohol task force.

Dealing with Resistance from the Alcohol Industry

The alcohol industry is complicated. One does not have to be cynical to view the industry's efforts to address the problem as mostly a public relations issue. Industry members typically point to something they are doing to address the problem and let themselves off the hook without impacting the business. Common examples include sober ride programs, voluntary practice agreements, and campaigns to market an image of responsibility. The reality is that the most effective strategies to reduce the negative social and health consequences of alcohol result in reduced sales volume—and revenues. So be prepared; many members of the industry are going to fight you.

One proactive policy is to not allow members of the alcohol industry to join the steering committee. They will use their influence to throw a wrench into the plans quickly. Insulate the steering committee from the industry, its money, and its lobbying muscle. An excellent article appeared in the *Wall Street Journal* in 2003 detailing the methods used by the industry to derail efforts to reduce binge drinking at Florida State University and should be required reading for every member of your team.[84] We have distilled it into a case example later in this chapter.

Your basic stance must be to limit the industry's influence on strategic decision processes and refocus its work in directions that are beneficial. For example, as noted above, the industry usually likes campaigns to check IDs, provide safe rides, monitor bad marketing messages, and provide public education. These programs *do* have a place. The key is to avoid letting those activities replace the ones that you know are more effective. (However, beware of "drink responsibly" campaigns, pushed by some wholesalers and manufacturers. These campaigns can be misleading in that often the underlying message is, "Drink.")

The American Medical Association has provided the following guidance on involving the alcohol business in the campus alcohol task force. (The suggestions below are adapted from the AMA publication *Partner or*

Foe? The Alcohol Industry, Youth Alcohol Problems, and Alcohol Policy Strategies.[85])

- The industry earns about 10 percent of its income from under-age drinkers. However, among college students, approximately half of the alcohol consumed is by those who are under the legal drinking age.[86] Even though seven of ten Americans drink very little or not at all,[87] the industry has been seeking to normalize alcohol consumption via its "educational messages" on responsible consumption. (The Distilled Spirits Council of the United States, for example, has stated that it seeks to ensure cultural acceptance of alcohol beverages by normalizing them in the minds of consumers as a healthy part of a normal lifestyle.)
- The industry also seeks to push all responsibility for problems on to consumers, rather than accept accountability for the producers, wholesalers, and retailers of a known potentially dangerous product. It invests heavily in fighting effective public health strategies that reduce the availability and raise the price of alcohol.
- The industry often seeks to sponsor alcohol prevention initiatives it prefers. These sponsorships help it generate a positive public image, defeat environmental policy proposals, create dependence (by becoming a key funder of the campus initiative), and influence the content of prevention programs.

The offer of money by an industry representative can trigger arguments among coalition members and divide them. To avoid this problem, consider the following steps:

Develop written policies stating from whom you will accept funding *before* you are offered money. Ground the policies in your university's and the group's philosophy and mission.

Develop a long-term, sustainable funding strategy for the coalition. Include a variety of funding sources and establish a plan for contacting them.

If you think you may need alcohol industry support, develop clear guidelines for accepting the funds. These should be set up to constrain the industry, prohibit use of the coalition's name, prohibit advertising, include environmental policy reforms, and maintain complete control over the program. The potential funder may well reject these constraints— which is a golden opportunity to expose the industry's public relations and political agendas.

CASE EXAMPLE

HOW THE ALCOHOL INDUSTRY DERAILS ALCOHOL PREVENTION

In late 1999, Florida State University (FSU) was named the top "party school" by the *Princeton Review* college guide. Research by the Harvard School of Public Health had shown that 53 percent of FSU students were binge drinkers, as compared to 44 percent nationwide. Shortly after, the university set up a coalition to reduce student alcohol abuse, called "The Partnership for Alcohol Responsibility," with help from a five-year Robert Wood Johnson Foundation grant. Goals included alcohol access reduction via ending ladies-drink-free nights and other discounts, prohibiting those under age twenty-one from entering bars, and increasing penalties for service to underage patrons.

The president of FSU offered committee membership to Susie Busch-Transou, the co-owner of a regional alcohol distributor and part of the famous Busch beer-brewing family. However, the committee blocked her appointment. Nevertheless, the owner attended most of the publicly held meetings, challenged the group's leaders, and challenged the group's attempts to limit discounts and impose regulations. Eventually, the alcohol industry formed

continued on next page

a rival group called "The Responsible Hospitality Council." Then Busch-Transou met with the president of FSU and offered to fund a "social norms" program. Social norms programs use educational materials such as posters to publicize surveys that show that most students drink in moderation, if at all. (Note that such data contradicted the reality that FSU already had a 53 percent binge-drinking rate.) Importantly, research shows that social norms marketing programs by themselves do not change heavy drinking at schools that try the approach.

Busch-Transou offered the school a $457,000 grant. The president accepted. Moreover, the president decided that FSU would not support any new state laws to limit youth drinking, damaging the Partnership for Alcohol Responsibility's plans to lobby for bills and contradicting the goals of the grant from the Robert Wood Johnson Foundation.

The alcohol funding drove a rift between the FSU president and the partnership. However, the partnership continued in its plans to limit access by ending underage access to bars, increasing penalties for serving underage drinkers, restricting alcohol marketing, and eliminating drink specials. Alcohol industry leaders worked to derail the plan, claiming it would raise alcohol prices and punish all drinkers—and reminding people that Prohibition had failed.

Eventually, the head of the partnership resigned. However, the binge-drinking rate climbed slightly, to 55 percent (per a Harvard School of Public Health survey), though the incidences of some types of alcohol-related harm declined.

The case, reported in the *Wall Street Journal,* is a clear example of how the alcohol industry actively blocks efforts to prevent binge drinking. It also shows why it is important to be careful about any connections between the alcohol task force and the alcohol industry. Finally, it shows the value of developing clear policies about accepting financial or other support from the alcohol industry *before* such support is offered.[88]

Chapter Summary

The research is clear: increasing the price of alcohol reduces its consumption, and reduces the negative consequences associated with it. The tactics described here are among the most effective things you can do to reduce student drinking and the consequences that result. Students are especially sensitive to price, and the more expensive alcohol becomes, the more likely they are to spend their money on less risky products and activities.

For college officials and the members of the alcohol task force, taking on the alcohol industry and local businesses to increase the price of alcohol is a tough task. However, it is one that is in the best interests of students, your university's mission, and the larger community where your school is located. The payoffs can be quite large: a reduction in the negative consequences of alcohol use, healthier students, and fewer dropouts.

There is reason for the alcohol task force to allow for development time before it tackles the issue of alcohol pricing near campus. The task force needs to gel as a team and generate a history of success. The activities necessary to raise prices—ending discounts and advocating for increased excise tax—are ambitious. People who join with you will be taking on a risk, and they need to know that you have a history of success. These advocacy efforts require political savvy and tremendous unity of purpose. But they are doable, and have the potential for great impact. As your group builds on its previous successes, it can prepare to work on these.

Afterword

Binge drinking at college is not new. As Henry Wechsler pointed out in his foreword to this book, Thomas Jefferson complained about drinking at the University of Virginia.

We appreciate that excessive drinking may be viewed by many, including some school officials, as a part of "the college experience." Yet the consequences of this "tradition" are severe. Students fail classes, they drop out, they make life-altering misjudgments, they injure themselves or others, and some die.

In this book, we have shown that binge drinking need not be a campus norm. (In fact, there are campuses where it is historically *not* the norm.) Binge drinking is dangerous, damaging, and inconsistent with a college's expectations of its students and its mission to aid their development and academic success.

We have made the facts about the consequences to students, to the college, and to the community clear, and we have provided strategies to change the campus community in ways that will reduce binge drinking. We have provided case examples of schools that have made significant changes in their drinking culture.

We are not neo-prohibitionists. We don't think alcohol is evil, and we don't want to get rid of alcohol. We are simply frank about it as a public health problem for college campuses. The consequences of binge drinking can be significant and severe; it can disrupt lives and impede students' ability to fulfill their promise.

But change is possible. Our goal through this book is to help the leaders on campus and in the surrounding community recognize that binge drinking occurs within a system of community standards and expectations, and to show how to shift those standards and expectations to reduce the frequency, prevalence, and negative consequences of binge drinking among students. That is, we see binge drinking on college campuses as a public health issue that can be dealt with through changes in college systems and the surrounding environment.

Our prescription for you is not *either-or;* it is *both-and.* Your campus must work to be sure it has appropriate interventions for students who develop alcohol disorders, *and* it must work to change community standards about how alcohol is served and consumed. The campus needs to attend to individual students and their problems, *and* it needs to change the policies, systems, rules, enforcement methods, alcohol availability, and other factors that contribute to a culture that either accepts or rejects student binge drinking.

We know that many readers of this book are already "with us" on this journey, and that for others, the idea may be new that binge drinking by college students merits a public health issue response. This book provides information, statistics, and carefully researched arguments to encourage a comprehensive and systematic approach that can be useful to all. A public health approach is consistent with a larger theme we think everyone can agree on: *Help students be successful by creating a community culture that reduces the influence of alcohol because that is best for our students.*

The specific policies and practices that we have described—many supported by considerable research evidence—have been reported elsewhere in various publications and papers cited throughout this book. Yet our book is unique in that we have synthesized and integrated this vast literature into a single, practical guide—one that offers a comprehensive and multidimensional plan for responding to the problem of student drinking. We have presented these as a series of steps, strategies, and tactics that move your campus and surrounding community toward a healthier environment regarding alcohol consumption by young people. This approach helps you build confidence with small successes as you prepare to tackle greater challenges. We are confident that if you act on the steps, strategies, and tactics described in this book, you will see progress with your goals. *They can work.*

If you have a prevention and intervention system in place, grounded in sound medical and environmental strategies, we hope that our book validates that you are on the right track. Perhaps we have raised areas in which you can further strengthen your practices and policies. For those campuses that have few, if any, services, we trust you will see our book as a guide toward the task of building a comprehensive system.

Designing and implementing a system to address college binge drinking is serious work. You will face numerous barriers, but patience and persistence will help you to achieve success. Be hopeful. The long journey begins with a single step. Starting down that path now will help you get there. The health of your students, the well-being of your community, and the reputation of your school are at stake.

Appendix: List of Documents on the CD-ROM

Document 1: Effectiveness of Alcohol Policies

Document 2: Sample Questions for Surveys of Your Task Force
Members/Stakeholder Group

Document 3: Program Evaluation Guide to the Collection of
Campus and Community Indicators

Document 4: Sample Public Opinion Survey Questions

Document 5: Screening Tools

Document 6: Comprehensive Assessment Tools

Document 7: Risk Management Policy for Campus Fraternities
and Sororities

Document 8: Keg Registration

Notes

1. H. Wechsler, J. E. Lee, M. Kuo, M. Seibring, T. F. Nelson, and H. Lee, "Trends in College Binge Drinking during a Period of Increased Prevention Efforts: Findings from Four Harvard School of Public Health College Alcohol Study Surveys: 1993–2001," *Journal of American College Health* 50 (2002): 203–17.

2. R. A. Grucza, K. E. Norberg, and L. J. Bierut, "Binge Drinking among Youths and Young Adults in the United States: 1979–2006," *Journal of the American Academy of Child and Adolescent Psychiatry* 48, no. 7 (2009): 692–702.

3. E. E. Bouchery, H. J. Harwood, J. J. Sacks, C. J. Simon, and R. D. Brewer, "Economic Costs of Excessive Alcohol Consumption in the U.S., 2006," *American Journal of Preventive Medicine* 41, no. 5 (2011): 516–24.

4. www.noellevitz.com/papers-research-higher-education/2009/2009-cost -recruiting-report; www.act.org/research/policymakers/pdf/retain_2011.pdf; www.nacada.ksu.edu/clearinghouse/advisingissues/retain.htm.

5. J. A. Martinez, K. J. Sher, and P. K. Wood, "Is Heavy Drinking Really Associated with Attrition from College? The Alcohol-Attrition Paradox," *Psychology of Addictive Behaviors* 22, no. 3 (2008): 450–56.

6. www.mndaily.com/2009/04/27/students-riot-dinkytown

7. www.mndaily.com/2003/04/14/hockey-win-fuels-another-riot-dinkytown

8. I. M. Newman, D. F. Shell, L. J. Major, and T. A. Workman, "Use of Policy, Education, and Enforcement to Reduce Binge Drinking among University Students: The NU Directions Project," *International Journal of Drug Policy* 17 (2006): 339–49.

9. www.unl.edu/scarlet/archive/2004/09/23/story3.html

10. *A Matter of Degree Advocacy Initiative* (monograph). October 2003. Princeton, NJ: Robert Wood Johnson Foundation. www.rwjf.org/files /research/111703amod.initiative.pdf.

11. R. Pratt, "Is 21-only Crackdown Working in Iowa City?" *The Gazette,* April 11, 2011. http://thegazette.com/conversations/is-21-only-crackdown -working-in-iowa-city/

12. Facts in the list are adapted from Campus Fact Sheet and Frequently Asked Questions about College Binge Drinking at www.alcoholpolicymd.com /alcohol_and_health/campus_fact_sheet.htm and www.alcoholpolicymd .com/alcohol_and_health/faqs.htm.

13. Based on American Psychiatric Association DSM-IV system.

14. A. Dorwaldt. 1999. "A Public Relations Nightmare." From report on hockey hazing at University of Vermont. "A Matter of Degree" program evaluation team. Harvard School of Public Health and Robert Wood Johnson Foundation.

15. Adapted from "4 Tiers," National Institute on Alcohol Abuse and Alcoholism, www.collegedrinkingprevention.gov/StatsSummaries/4tier.aspx.

16. E. R. Weitzman, T. F. Nelson, M. Seibring, and H. Wechsler, *Needing, Seeking and Receiving Treatment for Alcohol Problems in College. A Report to the Center for Substance Abuse Treatment, Substance Abuse and Mental Health Services Administration,* 2005, Harvard School of Public Health College Alcohol Study.

17. www.thecommunityguide.org/alcohol/index.html

18. T. F. Nelson, T. L. Toomey, D. J. Erickson, K. M. Lenk, and K. C. Winters, "Implementation of NIAAA College Drinking Task Force Recommendations: How Are Colleges Doing 6 Years Later?" *Alcoholism: Clinical and Experimental Research* 34, no. 10 (2010): 1687–93.

19. For more information about this perspective, see www.jsad.com/jsad/article /Studying_College_Alcohol_Use_Widening_the_Lens_Sharpening_the_Foc us/1462.html.

20. Adapted from *College Systems Model: Addressing Student Alcohol Use and Related Problems.* University of Minnesota School of Public Health, Alcohol Epidemiology Program. www.epi.umn.edu/alcohol/conceptmod/index.shtm.

21. E. R. Weitzman, T. F. Nelson, and H. Wechsler, "Taking Up Binge Drinking in College: The Influence of Person, Social Group and Environment," *Journal of Adolescent Health* 32 (2003): 26–35.

22. Adapted from *Broadening the Base of Treatment for Alcohol Problems* by the Institute of Medicine (Washington, D.C.: National Academy Press, 1990), 30.

23. Weitzman et al., *Needing, Seeking and Receiving Treatment for Alcohol Problems in College* (see note 16).

24. Weitzman et al., "Taking Up Binge Drinking in College" (see note 21).

25. H. Wechsler, Unpublished data, 2001, Harvard School of Public Health College Alcohol Study.

26. Weitzman et al., "Taking Up Binge Drinking in College" (see note 21) and Wechsler et al., "Trends in College Binge Drinking" (see note 1).

27. T. F. Nelson and H. Wechsler, "Alcohol and College Athletes," *Medicine and Science in Sports and Exercise* 33 (2001): 43–47; T. F. Nelson and H. Wechsler, "School Spirits: Alcohol and Collegiate Sports Fans," *Addictive Behavior* 28 (2003): 1–11.

28. Wechsler et al., "Trends in College Binge Drinking" (see note 1).

29. H. Wechsler and T. F. Nelson, "Relationship between Level of Consumption and Harms in Assessing Drink Cut-Points for Alcohol Research," *Alcoholism: Clinical and Experimental Research* 30, no. 6 (2006): 922–27.

30. Adapted from A. C. Wagenaar and C. L. Perry, "Community Strategies for the Reduction of Youth Drinking: Theory and Application," *Journal of Research on Adolescence* 4 (1994): 319–45.

31. For supporting evidence, see the following articles: E. R. Weitzman, T. F. Nelson, H. Lee, and H. Wechsler, "Reducing Drinking and Related Harms in College: Evaluation of the 'A Matter of Degree' Program," *American Journal of Preventive Medicine* 21, no. 3 (2004): 187–96; T. F. Nelson, E. R. Weitzman, and H. Wechsler, "The Effect of a Campus-Community Environmental Alcohol Prevention Initiative on Student Drinking and Driving: Results from the 'A Matter of Degree' Program Evaluation," *Traffic Injury Prevention* 6, no. 4 (2005): 323–30; and E. R. Weitzman, T. F. Nelson, and H. Wechsler, "Assessing Success in a Coalition-based Environmental Prevention Programme Targeting Alcohol Abuse and Harms: Process Measures from the Harvard School of Public Health 'A Matter of Degree' Programme Evaluation," *Nordisk Alkohol & Narkotikatidskrift* (English Supplement) 20 (2003): 141–49.

32. See www.jsad.com/jsad/article/Studying_College_Alcohol_Use_Widening _the_Lens_Sharpening_the_Focus/1462.html and http://chemicalhealth initiative.blogspot.com/2009/06/prevention-paradox-and-public-health.html.

33. The American Medical Association's media advocacy guidelines can be found at www.ama-assn.org/resources/doc/alcohol/amod_histories.pdf. The Midwest Academy offers general training in community organizing; see www.midwestacademy.com. The Pacific Institute for Research and Evaluation offers specific training in alcohol issues; see www.pire.org.

34. Examples of a public opinion survey and report are available at the Alcohol Epidemiology Program website. See www.epi.umn.edu/alcohol/pubopin /2002_REPORT.PDF and www.epi.umn.edu/alcohol/pubopin/charts _appendices.pdf.

35. K. C. Winters, T. Toomey, T. F. Nelson, D. Erickson, K. Lenk, and M. Miazga, "Screening for Alcohol Problems among 4-Year Colleges and Universities," *Journal of American College Health* 59 (2011): 350–57.

36. Based on information provided by the literature or by authors of the instruments.

37. P. K. Kokotailo, J. Egan, R. Gangnon, D. Brown, M. Mundt, and M. Fleming, "Validity of the Alcohol Use Disorders Identification Test in College Students," *Alcoholism: Clinical and Experimental Research* 28 (2006): 914–20.

38. Based on information provided by the literature or by authors of the instruments.

39. Weitzman et al., *Needing, Seeking and Receiving Treatment for Alcohol Problems in College* (see note 16).

40. K. M. Caldeira, S. J. Kasperski, E. Sharma, K. B. Vincent, K. E. O'Grady, E. D. Wish, and A. M. Arria, "College Students Rarely Seek Help Despite Serious Substance Use Problems," *Journal of Substance Abuse Treatment* (in press).

41. Weitzman et al., *Needing, Seeking and Receiving Treatment for Alcohol Problems in College* (see note 16).

42. Nelson et al., "Implementation of NIAAA College Drinking Task Force Recommendations" (see note 18).

43. Winters et al., "Screening for Alcohol Problems" (see note 35).

44. M. E. Larimer and J. M. Cronce, "Identification, Prevention and Treatment: A Review of Individual-focused Strategies to Reduce Problematic Alcohol Consumption by College Students," *Journal of Studies on Alcohol* suppl 14 (2002): 148–63; M. E. Larimer and J. M. Cronce, "Identification, Prevention, and Treatment Revisited: Individual-focused College Drinking Prevention Strategies 1999–2006," *Addictive Behaviors* 32 (2007): 2439–68.

45. S. T. Walters and C. Neighbors, "Feedback Interventions for College Alcohol Misuse: What, Why and for Whom?" *Addictive Behaviors* 30 (2005): 1168–82.

46. N. P. Barnett and J. P. Read, "Mandatory Alcohol Intervention for Alcohol-Abusing College Students: A Systematic Review," *Journal of Substance Abuse Treatment* 29 (2005): 147–58.

47. S. T. Walters, E. Miller, and E. Chiauzzi, "Wired for Wellness: e-interventions for Addressing College Drinking," *Journal of Substance Abuse Treatment* 29 (2005): 139–45.

48. K. B. Carey, L. A. J. Scott-Sheldon, M. P. Carey, and K. S. DeMartini, "Individual-level Interventions to Reduce College Student Drinking: A Meta-analytic Review," *Addictive Behaviors* 32 (2007): 2469–94.

49. W. R. Miller and S. Rollnick, *Motivational Interviewing: Preparing People for Change,* 2nd ed. (New York: Guilford Press, 2002).

50. Carey et al., "Individual-level Interventions to Reduce College Student Drinking" (see note 48); Larimer and Cronce, "Identification, Prevention, and Treatment Revisited" (see note 44).

51. Based on information provided by the literature or by authors of the programs.

52. C. W. Runyan, "Using the Haddon Matrix: Introducing the Third Dimension," *Injury Prevention* 4 (1998): 302–7

53. Adapted from a map developed by University of Minnesota Learning Collaborative on High-Risk Drinking, National College Health Improvement Project, 2011.

54. Ibid.

55. H. Wechsler and T. F. Nelson, "Will Making Alcohol More Available by Lowering the Minimum Legal Drinking Age Decrease Drinking and Related Consequences among Youth?" *American Journal of Public Health* 100, no. 6 (2010): 986–92.

56. Weitzman et al., "Reducing Drinking and Related Harms in College" (see note 31); Nelson et al., "The Effect of a Campus-Community Environmental Alcohol Prevention Initiative" (see note 31); E. R. Weitzman and T. F. Nelson, "College Student Binge Drinking and the 'Prevention Paradox': Implications for Prevention and Harm Reduction," *Journal of Drug Education* 34, no. 3 (2004): 247–65.

57. A. Dorwaldt. 1998. From report on the riot and its aftermath. "A Matter of Degree" program evaluation team. Harvard School of Public Health and Robert Wood Johnson Foundation.

58. Interfraternity Council (IFC)/Panhellenic Council (PHC) at the University of Minnesota—Twin Cities Risk Management Policy. http://begreek .theginsystem.com/images/stories/documents/council_and_ofsl _information/ifc_rm_policy.doc. Used with permission.

59. The website for the Nebraska training is http://eeando.unl.edu/rbst/ne/. Similar training could be established in your state.

60. For more details, see http://health.jocogov.org/docs/CHAP%20Binge %20Drinking%20One%20Pager.pdf. Also see www.globaldrugpolicy.com /Issues/Vol%203%20Issue%203/Reducing%20Youth%20Access.pdf.

61. Model Social Host Liability Ordinance with Legal Commentary and Resources. 2005. Center for the Study of Law and Enforcement Policy, Pacific Institute for Research and Evaluation (Ventura, CA: Ventura County Behavioral Health Department Publication). www.ca-cpi.org/SIG_subsite /SIG_Documents/Resources/VCL_MSHLO_web2.pdf

62. R. A. Hahn, J. L. Kuzara, R. Elder, R. Brewer, S. Chattopadhyay, J. Fielding, T. S. Naimi, T. Toomey, J. C. Middleton, and B. Lawrence, "Task Force on Community Preventive Services: Effectiveness of Policies Restricting Hours of Alcohol Sales in Preventing Excessive Alcohol Consumption and Related Harms," *American Journal of Preventive Medicine* 39, no. 6 (2010): 590–604. www.thecommunityguide.org/alcohol/limitinghourssale.html

63. See these guidelines at www.discus.org/pdf/61332_DISCUS.pdf.

64. This ordinance may also be viewed at www.epi.umn.edu/alcohol/sample/kegord.shtm.

65. In recent years, both Iowa City, Iowa, and Omaha, Nebraska, have pushed to gain local control as a way to exert better control over alcohol consumption. Useful articles on this may be viewed at www.dailyiowan.com/2010/11/30 /Metro/20239.html; www.projectextramile.org/; and www.unomaha.edu /ncenter/alcoholimpact.php.

66. J. Kearney. 2001. From report on bikini contest. "A Matter of Degree" program evaluation team. Harvard School of Public Health and Robert Wood Johnson Foundation.

67. Learn about University of Nebraska–Lincoln activities at www.nudirections .org/index.php and www.nudirections.org/laws_offcampus.php.

68. To learn more about service to intoxicated individuals, see www.nhtsa.gov /DOT/NHTSA/Traffic%20Injury%20Control/Articles/Associated%20Files/8 11142.pdf.

69. B. Woods. 2001. From report to the "A Matter of Degree" program evaluation. GT SMART Partnerships for Policy and Enforcement.

70. C. Einhorn, "Minnesota Bill Would Ban Limitless Drinking Specials," *New York Times,* January 20, 2008.

71. www.thecommunityguide.org/alcohol/increasingtaxes.html

72. A. Wagenaar, M. J. Salois, and K. A. Komro, "Effects of Beverage Alcohol Price and Tax Levels on Drinking: A Meta-analysis of 1003 Estimates from 112 Studies," *Addiction* 104, no. 2 (2009): 179–90.

73. Appendix 2 of *Last Call for High-Risk Bar Promotions That Target College Students: A Community Guide* by D. F. Erenberg and G. A. Hacker, Center for Science in the Public Interest, 1997, describes state laws and regulations prohibiting alcohol promotions. Though dated, and written prior to the widespread use of social media, the publication remains a valuable free resource for alcohol coalitions.

74. Drink Specials Restriction, www.tampatac.org/Policy.htm.

75. K. Stewart, *Strategies to Reduce Underage Drinking.* Pacific Institute of Research and Evaluation and U.S. Department of Justice Office of Juvenile Justice and Delinquency Prevention, 2009, p. 29. www.udetc.org/documents /strategies.pdf.

76. Samples adapted from Erenberg and Hacker, *Last Call for High-Risk Bar Promotions*, 25–27 (see note 73).

77. Nelson et al., "Implementation of NIAAA College Drinking Task Force Recommendations" (see note 18), http://onlinelibrary.wiley.com/doi /10.1111/j.1530-0277.2010.01268.x/pdf.

78. See *State Control of Alcohol: Protecting the Public's Health*, published May 2010 by the Marin Institute, for more supporting evidence.

79. The ordinance language, the study, and information about the ordinance can be viewed at http://alcoholjustice.org/campaigns/charge-for-harm /san-francisco-charge-for-harm.html.

80. For example, the strategy was effectively used by Minnesota governor Tim Pawlenty, who would not raise taxes but proposed and gained support for a 75-cents-per-pack "health impact user fee" on tobacco cigarettes as a means of increasing revenue and balancing the state budget.

81. J. I. Daley, M. A. Stahre, F. J. Chaloupka, and T. S. Naimi, "The Impact of a 25-Cent-per-Drink Alcohol Tax Increase: Who Pays the Tab?" *American Journal of Preventive Medicine* 42, no. 4 (April 2012): 382–89.

82. R. W. Elder, B. Lawrence, A. Ferguson, T. S. Naimi, R. D. Brewer, S. K. Chattopadhyay, T. L. Toomey, J. E. Fielding, and the Task Force on Community Preventive Services, "The Effectiveness of Tax Policy Interventions for Reducing Excessive Alcohol Consumption and Related Harms," *American Journal of Preventative Medicine* 38, no. 2 (2010): 225. See www.thecommunityguide.org/alcohol/EffectivenessTaxPolicy InterventionsReducingExcessiveAlcoholConsumptionRelatedHarms.pdf. Also see www.thecommunityguide.org/alcohol/increasingtaxes.html.

83. V. DeMarco, "Tobacco, Alcohol Tax Hikes Good for Maryland," *Frederick News Post*, June 5, 2011, http://healthcareforall.com/2011/06/tobacco -alcohol-tax-hikes-good-for-maryland/.

84. B. Gruley, "How One University Stumbled in Its Attack on Alcohol Abuse," *Wall Street Journal*, October 14, 2003, http://online.wsj.com/article /0,,SB106608568326890400,00.html.

85. J. F. Mosher, American Medical Association, 2002. See www.ama-assn.org /resources/doc/alcohol/partner_foe_brief.pdf.

86. H. Wechsler, J. E. Lee, T. F. Nelson, and M. Kuo, "Underage College Students'
    Drinking Behavior, Access to Alcohol and the Influence of Deterrence
    Policies: Findings from the Harvard School of Public Health College
    Alcohol Study," *Journal of American College Health* 50 (2002): 223–36.

87. Centers for Disease Control and Prevention, "Vital Signs: Binge Drinking
    Prevalence, Frequency, and Intensity among Adults—United States, 2010,"
    Morbidity and Mortality Weekly Report, January 10, 2012.

88. Gruley, "How One University Stumbled" (see note 84).

About the Authors

Toben F. Nelson

Toben F. Nelson, Sc.D., is with the Division of Epidemiology and Community Health at the University of Minnesota School of Public Health. He works with the Alcohol Epidemiology Program, the Tobacco Policy Research Program, the Minnesota Population Center, the Minnesota Obesity Center, and the Tucker Center for Research on Girls and Women in Sports. He also co-directs the Harvard School of Public Health College Alcohol Study (CAS).

Prior to joining the faculty of the University of Minnesota, he was a researcher with the Harvard Prevention Research Center and the Harvard Injury Control Center. He holds a Bachelor of Arts degree in Psychology and Physical Education from Hamline University, a Master of Science degree in Kinesiology from the University of Wisconsin–Madison, and a doctorate in Public Health from Harvard University.

Dr. Nelson studies public policy, substance use, physical activity, obesity, motor vehicle safety, and the health impacts of participation in organized sports. He has appeared on CNN Headline News and New England Cable News, and his work has been featured in the *New York Times,* the *Boston Globe, USA Today,* ESPN.com, and *Sports Illustrated* magazine. In 2008 his research was recognized by Thomson Reuters as among the most highly cited scientific studies of the decade on the topic of underage and college student drinking according to their Essential Science Indicators.

Ken C. Winters

Ken C. Winters, Ph.D., is a professor in the Department of Psychiatry at the University of Minnesota, director of the Center for Adolescent Substance Abuse Research, and a senior scientist with the Treatment

Research Institute in Philadelphia. He received his B.A. from the University of Minnesota and a Ph.D. in Psychology (Clinical) from the State University of New York at Stony Brook. His primary research interests are the assessment and treatment of addictions, including adolescent drug abuse and problem gambling. He is on the editorial board of the *Journal of Substance Abuse Treatment* and the *Journal of Child and Adolescent Substance Abuse,* and has received numerous research grants from the National Institutes of Health and various foundations. He was the 2008 recipient of the Research to Evidence-Based Practice Award from JMATE, a national organization on effective treatment for adolescents. Dr. Winters is a frequent speaker and trainer, and serves as a consultant to many organizations, including the Hazelden Foundation, The Partnership at Drugfree.org, the National Center for Responsible Gaming, and the Mentor Foundation (an international drug abuse prevention organization).